RINKS TO ARENAS
Ten years of British Ice Hockey

Alice O'Brien

Castle Publications
A Division of
Nottingham University Press
Manor Farm, Main Street, Thrumpton
Nottingham, NG11 0AX, United Kingdom

NOTTINGHAM

First published 1998
© Castle Publications

British Library Cataloguing in Publication Data
British Ice Hockey:
O'Brien, A

ISBN 1-897676-89-1

Typeset by Castle Publications, Nottingham
Printed and bound by The Cromwell Press, Trowbridge, Wiltshire

Acknowledgements

As each new season is reviewed there is always at least one player commenting on how much the game has changed since,... they began senior hockey,... since last time they played in the premier,... even since the last season was reviewed and this gave me the inspiration to look at British Ice Hockey through the eyes of those who entertain us week in, week out - the players themselves.

Such a concept was simply not possible without the support and enthusiasm of the featured players who all, without exception, gave of their time freely. It is a great honour to have eleven of the best players in British Ice Hockey so involved in this book. Each player talked knowledgeably about the sport and openly about their own experiences which was invaluable to me and hopefully makes this book an enjoyable and informative read. Every effort has been made to ensure that the events described herein are factually correct, any errors are due to the author entirely.

Thanks go to Mike Smith for his photographs, Vic Batchelder of *Ice Hockey News Review*, Stewart Roberts of *The Ice Hockey Annual* and Simon Potter of *Powerplay* magazine for the use of material from their publication, whilst Gordon Wade supplied the statistics.

I would also like to thank Simon Robinson and Sarah Keeling at Castle Publications for taking on this project.

Many other people have also helped me with this book and thanks are also due to them: Mike O'Connor (introductions to the players), John and Brenda Machin (thoughts and proof reading), Shaun Finnie (encouragement and enthusiasm), Andy Carson (box loads of programmes and magazines), Joanne Collins (guidance on players associations and import rules) and last, but by no means least, my long suffering husband Kevin for keeping me motivated, letting me use his computer all the time and keeping me fed and watered.

Introduction

In the 1930s and 40s Ice Hockey was a thriving sport in rinks all round the United Kingdom. Even into the 50s things looked rosy and in 1954-55 the British League was formed with Scottish and English clubs playing in the same league for the first time. The first year seemed very successful but the next saw the league reduced to just five teams as spiralling costs caught up with over-spending teams. By 1960 the league expired and Ice Hockey in the UK entered the twilight years.

Only five teams survived throughout the next sixteen years; Murrayfield Racers, Whitley Warriors, Fife Flyers, Glasgow Dynamos and the Durham Wasps. During those sixteen years new teams came and went.

In 1970 things began to change as a Southern Ice Hockey Association and a Southern League were formed. In 1978 Sunderland started a team and Richmond had a new team. Bradford staged its first Ice Hockey in 1979 and in 1980 Nottingham rose again, Streatham had a million-pound face lift and there were eighteen senior teams in England.

By 1982 the British Ice Hockey Association (BIHA) were able to announce a big deal with Thames TV and ITV. It was decided to re-form the British League, but bearing in mind the lessons of the past it was decided to split the league into sections to minimise travelling time and costs. When the 1986-87 season dawned, the BIHA announced that more teams than ever before in the history of the sport would be taking part in the British League, with major sponsors like Heineken and Norwich Union. But the old school still dominated, with Murrayfield Racers and Durham Wasps now having home grown talent to supplement the Canadian imports.

Then in 1988 the Cooper brothers, outstanding British players who had come up through the junior ranks at Durham, moved to a new team in a new building, the Cardiff Devils. With the benefit of hindsight this was seen by many to be the dawn of the new era in Ice Hockey, the Professional era, which has seen the arrival of smart new Arenas to replace cold, damp and rundown rinks.

In 1996 Superleague was introduced to British Ice Hockey. Some worry that the game is running ahead of itself and the free spending Superleague teams will self-destruct as the British League did all those years ago. The BIHA and then the Superleague failed to find sponsors for their product until season 98/99 and the arrival of Sekonda, and despite grand plans Superleague teams all admit to making losses in the first year. A lot has happened to British Ice Hockey in the last ten years.

This book looks at those changes through the eyes of those who were there on the ice as it happened, the players themselves.

> In 1988 when the Cooper Brothers moved, did any British player ever imagine they would be able to make a real living playing Ice Hockey in the UK?

Did any player envisage playing in a venue like Manchester Arena?

Is Superleague the way to go, is it a new beginning or the beginning of the end for British Ice Hockey talent?

What events and people have shaped the British Ice Hockey scene over the last ten years?

This book is not the view of a historian looking in, nor the opinions of owners and officials, *this is the views of the players themselves.*

Season 1988/89

with

David Graham

British goalie for the Nottingham Panthers

	GPI	MINS	SHOTS	GA	GAA
HEINEKEN CHAMPIONSHIP	5	272	181	23	5.07
HEINEKEN LEAGUE	29	1675	977	140	5.01
NORWICH UNION CUP	8	440	292	39	5.32
EUROPEAN CHAMPS POOL D	3	150	N/AV	12	4.80

HEINEKEN CHAMPIONS: NOTTINGHAM PANTHERS

PREMIER DIVISION: DURHAM WASPS

NORWICH UNION CUP: DURHAM WASPS

Chapter One

In 1988 two things happened which changed the face of British Ice Hockey for ever. Firstly, two young British brothers, Ian and Stephen Cooper, who had come up through the junior ranks of the Durham Wasps, were signed by Cardiff Devils Ice Hockey Club to play ice hockey as professionals some three hundred miles from home. The move saw the brothers move from a club with an outstanding history at the top level to a club which was in its third season and a division lower than the Wasps. Secondly, Alex Dampier, then coach of the Nottingham Panthers decided to sign one foreign forward and two defencemen. Each British team was allowed to sign three foreign players, called 'imports' and the choice previously had always been to sign two goalscorers and one man for defence. Top British goalie at the time, David Graham, believes that as well as helping the Panthers that year, Alex's change was to have a huge impact on the British game in the future.

> 'That helped the team because it's always been, in this country, how many goals you could get and that was basically it. You just out-scored the other team, you never really thought about defensive hockey. Then Alex brought two defencemen in and that began to change the whole game.'

David Graham, was also signed by defensively minded Alex Dampier ready for the 1988/89 season. David, another British talent from the North-East, was brought up opposite Whitley Bay Ice Rink and went to skate at the age of ten and got involved with ice hockey. Bob Gilbert was a Great Britain netminder based in Whitley Bay so David approached him to borrow the kit and started playing in goal. Why in goal?

> 'The main thing was everybody told me I was too tall, so that was my main incentive, to show everybody wrong. That was the way I was. I always wanted to play in goal, that was where the action was and you were always in the thick of it. My brother played in goal for Whitley Bay as well, so when we trained we always pushed each other to the limit. My mother used to have nightmares with us both playing in goal but it worked out well. My favourite NHL player was Ken Dryden, who was with Montreal Canadiens at the time, because he was 6'4" so I always followed Ken Dryden. That's why I wore 29 because Ken Dryden wore 29.'

After an appearance in a England team at an exhibition game in Solihull, David was asked by Gary Newbon to play for Solihull where he stayed for four seasons before Alex Dampier asked him to move to Nottingham. Although David was not paid a proper 'wage' to play, an amount to cover 'expenses' was paid.

> 'I was working in the fruit and veg market in Birmingham. I'd start about four in the morning and finish about one o'clock in the afternoon. Sometimes when we played in Scotland [Sunday] we'd get back at two in the morning [Monday] and I would drive straight to Birmingham and start work! It was tiring at times but I had to do it, it was all part of the job. It was a hard season but I had worked for seven years in the market and I enjoyed it. I'd work on Saturday morning before a home game, try and get off early, come home, get a couple of hours sleep and then head to the rink. By the end of the warm-up I was just about awake: some people might think it was later in the game!'

Nottingham Ice Stadium was designed as a scaled down version of the Harringay Arena and opened in the first wartime season 1940. The Nottingham Panthers made their debut against the Canadians of RAF (Grantham) and lost 7-4. That first Nottingham squad was: Torgalson, Spencer, J Block, R Block, Brown, Rivett, Lee, Max Keller, White, Jones and Raines. One of Nottingham's best players in ice hockey's glory days was Victor 'Chick' Zamick who won the scoring title in 1950/51 together with the league's most popular player and was voted Sportsman of the year in Nottingham against cricketers Reg Simpson and Joe Hardstaff and channel swimmer Tim Blower. 'Chick' went on to coach the Nottingham team in 1955. When he had arrived in Nottingham Victor was described as a skinny, undersized, undernourished Ukrainian youngster, who only got his chance to come to Britain when another player pulled out 48 hours before the new imports were due to leave Canada by ship.

Nottingham were out of hockey from 1960 until 1980 when Gary Keward, who was managing Sheffield Lancers, successfully negotiated to bring the sport back to Nottingham. Many of the Sheffield team followed him down the motorway including his son Dwayne who had been Lancers leading scorer.

Expected to do well in the Premier Division in the 1988/89 season were Murrayfield Racers who were longing to take their third league title in a row and Durham Wasps who could take their third play-off Championship title in a row. Having lost the valuable Cooper brothers to Cardiff, the Wasps announced that this season would be a time of rebuilding, but few would expect them to be far off the pace. Every team was allowed three imports so it was often the best British players that made the difference. Durham always had a strong junior development for bringing through young British players like the Cooper brothers, Ian and Stephen, and the Johnson brothers, Shaun, Anthony and Stephen, to strengthen the team.

Two new teams in two new arenas joined ice hockey at ELD1 (English League Division One). The Basingstoke Beavers played in the Playground rink with the first game being a challenge match on July 17th between the Beavers and Bournemouth Sharks, Beavers won 27-2! The Humberside Ice Arena became home to the Humberside Seahawks whose first game was 18th September in the English League Cup against the Solihull Knights, Humberside won 13-4. Humberside Seahawks go on to win English League Division One, whilst Basingstoke finished fourth.

The Ice Hockey season starts with the first rounds of the Autumn Cup, sponsored in 1988 by Norwich Union. The teams are divided into three regional groups: England North, England South and Scotland. Top of the table in England North is the Durham Wasps, winning all eight games played in the group stage. Nottingham came third in the England North division. David Graham started well with a shut out of the Cleveland Bombers on the second weekend. David was certainly proud of his Cup shut-out but doesn't take all the credit.

'It's a team effort if you get a shut-out - particularly your defence - and you are the last line of defence. Terry Kurtenbach and 'Doc' Durdle did really well. Terry K, there is a sixty minute man, he broke his jaw one year, put a mask on and still played. They had to play because there was only three of you, so it was a case of getting strapped up and back out there.'

4

Peterborough Pirates start the season well topping the England South group, dropping only one game at home to Telford by eleven goals to ten. Unfortunately for Peterborough their league chances took a knock in the cup when Paul Heavey gets a ten match ban for a challenge directly from a face off on Solihull Barons import Denis Bourque which left the import with a facial injury. This altercation took place directly after Solihull goalie Brian Cox took exception to being scored against and was sent for the early shower.

Although the cup campaign began well for Nottingham, lone forward Bruce Thompson was working hard but struggling to find the net. In the eight games of the first round in the cup Bruce scored six and had 17 points compared with 'defenceman' Darren 'Doc' Durdle who had scored 17 and notched up a total of 27 points. It certainly wasn't easy being an import.

> 'What happened then was you wanted the imports to score the goals, stop the goals and do all the fighting, so they got paid for everything. They had to do everything and there was a lot of pressure on the imports. If they didn't score three or four goals a game then they were getting asked why not and they were on the ice for fifty minutes. It was a lot harder then, they had to earn their money.'

Coach Alex Dampier surprised many when he stuck with the new system and brought in Paul Adey as lone import forward to replace Thompson, but things started to click almost as soon as Adey arrived. David Graham was impressed.

> 'Paul Adey could play alongside the young British lads, the likes of Simon Hunt and Simon Perkins. Gavin Fraser was also one of the more experienced players and Nigel Rhodes. Paul fitted in really well and worked with them. I know it must have been frustrating at times for Paul but the British played really well alongside him.'

Only one other shut-out occurred in the Norwich Union Cup that year. Tayside Tigers with the help of goalie Gerry Anderson shut-out Glasgow on their way to the final. The two winners from the English groups of the cup, Peterborough and Durham, played to see who faced the Scottish winners, Tayside Tigers. The first game on 18th October sees Peterborough Pirates fight back from a 1-6 first period to tie the game at 7-7 in front of a capacity crowd of 2,200 people. The Durham leg on 25th October sees the first period again go to the Durham Wasps 7-2, but this time the Pirates cannot stage another come back and eventually go down 17-3 in front of a sell-out 2,800 fans.

Durham Wasps went on to beat the Tayside Tigers 7-5 in the final of the Cup played in Birmingham at the National Exhibition Centre's Hall 5 in front of 3,580 fans on December 3rd. The final was televised by the BBC on Grandstand with Paul Ferguson and Red Imrie commentating.

In January Nottingham played reigning Champions Murrayfield Racers. The game was featured on Grandstand as 'Game of the Month.' Playing in front of the cameras was special for players at that time.

'It was nice to be on the TV and everyone appreciated what was going on at the time, because a lot of us were working as well, so you could say to your mates I'll be on the TV Saturday afternoon. And then you'd be there Monday morning "did you see it?" and they'd say " oh yeah, you were rubbish..." or "you played well" depending on whether you won or lost!'

David Graham between the pipes for Nottingham

January was also the month that Gary Unger, the most experienced ex-NHL player in the country was sacked as coach of the Peterborough Pirates (The NHL in Canada – the National Hockey League - is recognised as the best ice hockey league in the world). David thinks Gary's professional experience, in this instance, probably worked against him.

'With Gary, he came from a totally professional set-up and the trouble is in them days there were three foreigners who were playing golf and a couple of British lads who might be getting paid, but eighty or ninety percent of your team were *working. So Gary would say, "we're training at this time" and most of the lads would say "I can't turn up, I'm working." That happened all through the league but I think that was the main reason. Training had always been when the session finished at half past ten at night, so everybody could make that but then they started to say "oh well we'll train dinner times or tea time" and a lot of your team can't make it.'*

Import Chris McCauley, assisted by Todd Bidner, added the role of coaching to their roles as players for Peterborough.

Young British Player of the Year 1989/90:
Anthony Johnson of Durham Wasps

Each year a 'Young British Player of the Year' is voted for by the coaches in the Premier Division. The overall winner gets to attend a two week training Camp for the Calgary Flames, courtesy of that organisation, the Government of Alberta, Canadian Airlines International and the Ice Hockey News Review. Anthony Johnson is the fourth winner of this annual award.

'These guys are going to training camp, to make the grade, so you are not messing about, he went there for a training camp and he was trying to get there [NHL]. I've never been so I just imagine the standard of the kids there would be immense. It shows that the kids can do it, training once or twice a week on a late night Tuesday/Thursday night, not like the Superleague where they train everyday.'

David Graham on Anthony Johnson
'He was a hard worker, it was a family ethic that they all worked really hard, he put in a lot of effort as did his brothers and his Dad. Anthony got a lot of respect for it, for putting in 100% and I'm sure it rubbed off on a lot of the other Durham players. At the time Durham were at the high point of the game and that came down to the Coopers and the Johnsons.'

In February the Cardiff Devils beat Medway Bears 8-5 to virtually clinch the Division One title. Over the season they were never beaten in the Wales National Ice Rink and suffered only two defeats on the road. It was not all plain sailing for the Devils as Medway Bears kept them on their toes, finishing just one point behind them after drawing with Telford Tigers. According to Andy Weltch in *The Ice Hockey Annual* for that year John Lawless had:

" ...infuriated certain factions of British ice hockey's establishment by offering the British stars a share of the sport's profits. He was accused of 'cheque book hockey' and warned of the dangers of professionalism, but he hit back with claims that the more established clubs were simply scared of the inevitable course the sport was taking."

The balance of power had begun to shift from those who could develop talent to those who could pay for talent. Certainly David Graham saw Cardiff's move to sign the British Cooper brothers, as professional British players, merely as a continuation of what had gone before.

'Nottingham, really, were the first money team, there were a couple of players getting expenses and then Cardiff went totally professional with bringing the Cooper brothers down to Cardiff, and then it just went on from there. Cardiff had some professional players and then they had a good development there and started bringing the local lads into it.'

On February 18th at Whitley Bay, Murrayfield's Tony Hand, the only British Player to have been drafted to play on an NHL team, scored his 1,000[th] Heineken League Point. The 1,000[th] point was an assist on a Louis Haman goal at 32.33 in the game.

In March Durham Wasps win their second trophy of the year and their third Heineken league title with an 12-1 home win over Ayr whilst last year's champions, Murrayfield Racers, experienced a shock defeat 13-12 at Streatham who were propping up the wrong end of the league table.

Heineken British League Premier Division	GP	W	L	D	GF	GA	Pts
Durham Wasps	36	26	6	4	371	246	56
Murrayfield Racers	36	25	9	2	404	266	52
Nottingham Panthers	36	22	9	5	305	193	49
Fife Flyers	36	24	11	1	311	231	49
Whitley Warriors	36	22	12	2	347	266	46
Ayr Bruins	36	17	15	4	285	273	38
Peterborough Pirates	36	9	23	4	268	331	22
Solihull Barons	36	9	24	3	228	386	21
Tayside Tigers	36	7	26	3	236	331	17
Streatham Redskins	36	4	30	2	221	453	10

Durham Wasp Rick Brebant is top of the scorers for the Premier Division with 99 goals and 218 points. Tony Hand of the Murrayfield Racers is in second place with 86 goals and 212 points. (In ice hockey a point is awarded for a goal scored and for an assist, which is a pass that leads to a goal scored by another player). Leading netminder in the league is David Graham who faced 977 shots and let in 140 goals, giving a 'goals against' average of 5.01. The two Fife Flyers netminders take second and third place Craig Dickson with 6.24 goals against and Martin Mckay with 6.40. The top four penalty minute (Pims) takers came from just two clubs. Dave Ross of Whitley accumulated 133 minutes, just behind him is team mate Mike Rowe who was penalised 122 Pims, next came two Ayr players with 114 and 112 Pims.

The 16th to 21st of March saw a Great Britain team in action at the World and European Championships for the first time in seven years. The Pool D tournament was staged in Belgium at Geel and Heist op-den-Berg. The British team only lost one game on the ice drawing with Romania 6-6 and losing by the narrowest of margins 6-5 to the host nation, but many were disappointed with the performance and some voiced concerns about complacency and a lack commitment.

'A lot happens on the day of a game, especially at the World Championships. We all went over to play, and to play to the best of our ability, but it was the first time we'd all been together at that sort of level. Nerves come in and some people might have been upset about their ice time. I wouldn't say anybody was complacent but you can't make excuses: when you're out there you've got to play. I personally think we all went out there to do the job and I was deeply disappointed that we didn't do better. Because I played a lot I took it on myself that we should have done better. I won best goal keeper of the tournament, it totally shocked me, I'm standing in the line up and when they said it I wasn't expecting it at all. When I got it, it was really, really nice, but I think I would have preferred to hand that in and win the gold, or for the team to have done better because they deserved it. There was a lot of criticism from these people who always criticise the British team but you don't, as a sportsman, you don't go out there to do bad. You don't go out there to have a bad game, these things happen.'

The World Championships were a tough learning experience for many British players. Tony Hand was one of the British players singled out for criticism after he turned up for one game without his helmet, whilst in another he asked for his skates to be sharpened just prior to the start of the game and missed some of the first period as his skates are not sharpened but further blunted by the local rink staff. By the end of the tournament, however, it was Tony who won the organiser's award for the tournament's best forward.

World & European Championship Pool D	GP	W	L	D	GF	GA	Pts
Belgium	4	3	1	0	35	9	6
Romania	4	2	1	1	69	7	5
Britain	4	1	2	1	19	16	3
Spain	4	1	3	0	29	27	2
New Zealand	4	0	4	0	3	96	0

Stranger things were to follow. A month after the championships the Belgians informed the IIHF (International Ice Hockey Federation) that *all* players tested for drugs on the first day of the tournament had tested positive. However the players concerned were cleared, and the testing brought into question when it became apparent that the players, from several different nations, had exactly the same amounts of exactly the same banned substance in their samples!

It seems, reading between the lines, that the critics who didn't want to see the British players turn professional in the league, nevertheless expected a highly professional unit when the same people took leave from their employers and turned out for their country for the first time in seven years.

'There was a lot of pressure on kids then, like I say we had two jobs. All of a sudden you're in the Great Britain team and there was never enough time to train. I remember me and Nigel Rhodes had to go up to Durham and when we get up to Durham the Zamboni [which resurfaces the ice] has broken down on the ice so we just went up there, got a team photo and then came back, you just couldn't believe half of it.'

9

Would imports have made a difference to that team?

'Imports wouldn't have made a difference at that time. Of course it would have been different with imports, but its just Terry Matthews went with the team that he thought would be the best team and Terry was a British guy and he wanted to go and try and prove a point. Of course everyone was quick to attack him when he got back and I guess that's when Alex [Dampier] took over.'

Even now David Graham holds some firm beliefs about British Ice Hockey and the British team.

'We are not a small Canada we're British. It really annoys me when we are letting Canadians run our British hockey. I take my hat off to Paul Heavey, the only British kid in Superleague [coaching Cardiff] and I think Paul's doing a fantastic job there. Paul's been around enough and he should be given the job [GB coach]. I know we'll use Canadian players but it will be British style with a British coach.'

That year the British team members came home from Belgium and back to their teams for the Championship play-offs.

'Usually we went straight after Wembley but that year World Championships was before. We trained every day and I came back to Wembley feeling really good.'

The top six teams in the Premier League go into the Wembley play-offs whilst the bottom team, Streatham Redskins, enter promotion/relegation playoffs with the top team in Division One, the Cardiff Devils. The Cardiff Devils win the first encounter at the Wales National Ice Rink 12-1 on 2nd April. Things were little better for Streatham on April 9th when Cardiff beat them 5-9 at home. Cardiff gain promotion with an emphatic 21-6 aggregate score.

For the Wembley finals, coach of the sixth placed Ayr Bruins, Rocky Saganiuk, was confidently predicting a Nottingham/Ayr championship final at Wembley on the 22nd April.

In Group A of the quarter finals the Fife Flyers failed to make it to Wembley when they were on the wrong side of a shut-out as Whitley Bay netminder Kevin Dean stopped all 40 shots on goal to take only the third shut-out in play-off history (9-0). It was the first time Fife had failed to make it to Wembley since 1984. Durham Wasps and Whitley Bay progressed to the semi-finals at Wembley, from Group A.

In Group B another Scottish side, Murrayfield Racers, also failed to make it to Wembley. Murrayfields only points came from their first game at home to Nottingham. They looked on target when the home game with Ayr was poised at 4-4 but then Ref Ed Miller called a match penalty on Tony Hand for fighting and the Bruins went on to win 8-5. Then Murrayfield went to Nottingham needing a win to qualify for Wembley.

'That was a huge game, because Alex used to coach there, and especially against Tony Hand who always gives you something to work with. When Tony and Scott Neil were there it was always good to shut Tony down because he could score at

will and it was always a challenge. The way I used to play my game was to challenge myself against the better players, like Tony. I think that's why I have done well because I always tried to keep the best ones out and stop them from scoring.'

Although in the same play-off group, Ayr and Nottingham only met once in earnest in the quarter finals because by their second meeting both had qualified for their Wembley semi-final places. In the first meeting though, David Graham came within minutes of shutting out the Bruins.

'Concentration was always my game, and I always panicked towards the end of the game that I wanted the game to finish. The last two or three minutes I'd start to freeze. You learn from experience and it was just nice to get to play at Wembley. As long as you win the game, that's the way I looked at it.'

Nottingham won that game 7-1.

By making it to the Wembley weekend Nottingham Panthers had got further than ever before in the modern play-off championship and most fans went to Wembley already satisfied with their club's achievements. Most of the pundits expected one of the North East teams, Durham or Whitley to take the Championship.

The first semi final was on April 22nd at 1pm and saw Whitley Warriors beaten 6-8 by the Panthers. Kevin Dean played in the nets for Whitley, but back-up netminder for the Warriors was David's brother Peter. Our photograph shows the two brothers on the ice together straight after that game.

'You can see the pads I had were repaired. If you did that now the kids wouldn't wear them. Most of my equipment I'd pass on to my brother. Often we paid weekly. It wasn't just the cost, it was basically you were given the equipment that was there. It was always Koho sticks and that was it. It was the same with the equipment, you could have "this" and that was it. Then I started using this stuff, John Brown, that's what all my equipment was, and then it was always Cooper and then Vaughn come in. Now you can pick your own.'

The second semi final faced off at 6.30pm and the lowly sixth in the league Ayr Bruins beat the Championship title holders 12-6, Durham Wasps failing in their attempt to make it a hat trick of wins and take the Grand Slam. The Ayr players played like men possessed. Danny Shea, the import forward brought in to replace Rocky on the ice when he decided to concentrate on coaching, won over many new fans, with a five goal personal performance. 8,800 fans saw this exciting performance, 100 more than had seen the earlier game.

The final was the next day. Before the Senior Championship final the Junior C Championship final is contested between the Scottish Champions and the English Champions with the winner taking the title of British Junior League Champions. This year the junior final was decided on penalty shots, after which Nottingham Panthers took on the Ayr Bruins in the senior final. Nico Toeman, chief referee, was in charge with linesmen Paul Branch and Gordon Pirry, in front of 8,996 eager ice hockey fans.

11

Peter and David Graham at the Wembley finals

British Junior League Championship
April 23rd Wembley

Durham Mosquitoes 5   Dundee Bengals.......5   (4-0, 0-3, 1-2)
Mosquitoes won on penalty shots 4-1
Durham Goal Scorers: Walker 2, Dixon 1+2, Johnson 1+2, Wright 1,
Penalty shots: Walker, Tasker, Dixon, O'Connor
Dundee Goal Scorers: Haig 2+2, Kern 1+1, Smith 1+1, Charles 1
Penalty shots: Haig
Attendance 4,000

The destination of the Championship trophy was in doubt until the last period of the last game. The first period one a piece; the second period two each, but the Bruins had given their all to beat Durham the evening before. Nottingham sensed victory was theirs and unanswered goals from Terry Kurtenbach, Gavin Fraser and Randell Weber gave them the Championship title on their first visit to the Wembley finals.

Coach of the Year (one of the British Ice Hockey Writers Association awards) went to Alex Dampier in the Premiership.

> 'Alex does well. Like all coaches you've got to stick to your guns and do what you think and at the time in Nottingham we had a very young squad so we played that system and it worked out well.'

The season was also a very good one for David Graham, being top of the goalie stats. He was also voted "all star goalie" by the Writers Association. Closer to home he won a few awards in Nottingham.

> 'I think I won Player of the Year at Nottingham, and won most consistent player at Nottingham. It was just a really good year.'

Season 1989/90

with

Ian & Stephen Cooper

British players for the
Cardiff Devils

Ian Cooper – Forward	GP	G	A	Pts	PIM
Heineken Championship	6	8	9	17	14
Heineken League	32	48	53	101	94
Norwich Union Cup	10	26	19	45	28
Totals	**48**	**82**	**81**	**163**	**136**

Stephen Cooper – Defenceman	GP	G	A	Pts	PIM
Heineken Championship	6	4	2	6	10
Heineken League	30	19	40	59	47
Norwich Union Cup	10	2	12	14	26
Totals	**46**	**25**	**54**	**79**	**83**

HEINEKEN CHAMPIONS: Cardiff Devils

PREMIER DIVISION: Cardiff Devils

NORWICH UNION CUP: Murrayfield Racers

Chapter Two

So why had the Coopers moved to Cardiff in Division One last year? Younger brother, Ian said:

> 'We were on little more than expenses at Durham and come the end of that season we'd heard rumours that other players were getting decent wages and we thought there was an opportunity that we could move from Durham and get a decent wage. So we went in and approached Tom Smith and asked if we could have a raise in our money, and he laughed at us.'

Stephen added:

> 'He said he would never pay a British player to play. I think that was his exact wording. So when John Lawless gave us the opportunity we decided to grab it with both hands and that is why we're here.'

For the Cooper brothers and their Cardiff team mates the pre-season "Trafford Tournament" was a significant highlight and good indicator of how their season would go this year. It took place at the Altrincham rink on Monday 28th August 1989.

> Ian: 'Everyone thought the standard in Division One was so bad that a team coming up into Premier just wouldn't cut it. We were going to be the whipping dogs from Division One and that was our first outing as a Premier team. We were playing in a one-day tournament with other Premier teams and at the end of the day we walked away winning that with a big cheque in the pocket.'

> Stephen: 'Because we didn't actually change the team, we kept the same team. We were so nervous, and first team up was Durham, our old team. So it was a nerve racking game but we got off to a great start in the competition, and the whole season. We beat Durham in the first game 4-0 in two twenty minute periods.'

Whilst Cardiff beat Durham to get into the next round, home team Trafford put out Bracknell Bees, Solihull Barons beat Peterborough Pirates and went on to beat Trafford in the next round and Nottingham, after putting out Whitley, were then put out by Cardiff in the next round. The final played between Solihull and Cardiff was played over the normal three periods. Solihull may have wished it was shorter after Cardiff took a 4-0 lead in the first period, but Solihull pulled back in a 1-4 second period before Cardiff went on to take the third 2-0 and win the game 7-4.

> Ian: 'We beat Durham, Whitley Bay, Nottingham. That was a big shock and that's when the odds started coming down. We started the year 100-1, we went to 66-1, then 33-1, a few people in the club and lots of supporters had money on us. Some supporters say they won £20,000 off the double 100-1 on each competition.'

The Norwich Union Cup kicks off the start of the season proper in September. The teams are divided into three regional groups with the Scottish teams in one group and the other two being England North and England South (with a little bit of Wales).

Murrayfield take the Scottish Group (winning 4 games) ahead of Ayr Raiders. Durham lead England North whilst Solihull Barons finish second despite clocking up the same points (both winning 5 games). Cardiff Devils run away with England South winning eight games out of eight played. The two 'English' teams play-off home and away to decide who is to meet Murrayfield in the final.

On 8th September the BIHA announced that the Tayside Tigers were to withdraw from the Premier Division. The team had played all the previous season with the threat of the rink closing, but they thought their future was secure when Richard Williams became the new rink chairman. New owners and new promises fail to see the rink re-open after the summer and the Tayside Tigers are no more.

Highlight of Whitley Warriors season comes early, in those Norwich Union Cup games, as import Hilton Ruggles scores seven goals in just over eleven minutes (11.03), three of those arrived in one minute and eleven seconds, as Warriors beat Nottingham Panthers. Nottingham Panthers were struggling at the beginning of the season as both All-Star goalie David Graham and rushing defenceman Doc Durdle had both moved on during the summer. Durdle's replacement was Yves Beaudoin who was a defensive defenceman. The team missed Durdle's goal scoring input. David Graham was having a disappointing time down the road at Peterborough and he returned to Nottingham in October.

Whilst the Norwich Union Cup progressed, the league games begin and Cardiff go unbeaten in their first four games and take the top of the league table by the end of October.

> Stephen: *'I remember after about nine games we were talking about the unbeaten run but…'*
> Ian: *'another telling time was the first weekend.'*
> Stephen: *'Yeah, the Ayr, Murrayfield double header…'*
> Ian: *'so we couldn't have had a bigger test. We played...'*
> Stephen: *'Ayr first and tied, when Ayr were playing out of Glasgow.'*
> Ian: *'We got three points from the whole weekend and that was deemed to be a huge success going up there. That set us up for the rest of the year because we knew we could get the points off anyone.'*

That first weekend saw Cardiff play Ayr in Glasgow and draw 5-5 on the 7th October and the next night play Murrayfield Racers in Murrayfield, winning that one 8-3. Steve Moria scored 6+2 for Cardiff in the Murrayfield game. If anyone had any doubts about the newly promoted Devils, the Trafford Tournament, the first weekend of the league season and their emphatic top of the table in the England South Group left no-one in any doubt that the new team were going to be a force to be reckoned with.

October also sees the appointment of Alex Dampier as coach of the British team and the change of policy to include dual national players on the team. Dual nationals were mainly Canadians who had spent five years playing in this country and then qualified for a British Passport.

Ian Cooper playing for Great Britain

At the domestic level of the game a player needs to have played at junior level in this country to be a non-import or British player. Dual Nationals became a new category called "reclassified players", which meant some teams could sign an 'extra' import. Cardiff player manager, John Lawless, was one such player who had played as one of three imports. He gained the re-classified tag in the summer, thus making way for a new import in the team and the prompt signing of Doug McEwen.

Ian: *'The domestic scene was changing along those lines and eventually the laws would be changed and that's progressed to where we are today. Our view was, we're not making the rules, we've just got to play by the rules and if there are imports coming in, then we've just got to raise our game, or strengthen our game, to keep up with the quality of import coming in and that meant the quality of the dual nationals in the GB team. Its just fighting for your place against someone else, that's all.'*

Stephen: *'Plus all the other European nations were using dual national players. It was the only way for Britain to progress from D Pool to C and B Pools and get the status of ice hockey in Britain on to a higher plane and I think Alex helped a lot to do that.'*

Then came the two game England final of the Norwich Union Cup. The first leg was in Durham and the Wasps won convincingly 12-4. Whilst Cardiff had player-manager John Lawless sent for the early shower for fighting. The second game in Cardiff was six nights later. The Durham team decided to fly to the Welsh Capital, but unfortunately the 30 seater plane hit 75mph winds and was forced to land at Birmingham, from where the team had to travel by more conventional means, on a coach, arriving some three hours late for the game.

Stephen: *'We were down something like an eight goal deficit from the Durham leg and we nearly brought it back, we got up six goals at one point, when we finally got to play the game.'*

Ian: *'We had our equipment on, hanging around. Some of the boys went on to the ice for spells, sort of in fancy dress, half kitted up. It was like a scene from "Slapshot", dancing round and waltzing with each other, that was mainly Brian Dickson and Brian Wilkie.'*

Stephen: *'Bearing in mind that the crowd had also been there for four hours and they were starting to get a bit bored and no-one knew if the game would just get abandoned.'*

On the 19th November Whitley stage the battle of the Bay as well as a hockey match. First the hockey match which the visitors Ayr Raiders are winning 9-4 when the battle begins with 21 seconds left on the clock. When order is restored the game is abandoned as the Ayr team have only two players left on the ice with 17 match penalties called against the team. The tally of 371 penalty minutes is a new league record. Only five match penalties are upheld at the enquiry, Raiders are fined £1,000 and coach Rocky Saganiuk is suspended for a month and Ayr player Colin McHaffie for the rest of the season.

Young British Player of the Year: Iain Robertson of Fife Flyers

Ian and Stephen Cooper on Iain Robertson

Ian
'Quite underrated, fast skilful player, very good, very talented. Possibly a little bit too small which might have hindered him in later years.'

Stephen
'He might have furthered his career in recent years by making the move to England, but he is reluctant to do so. Staying in Fife possibly held him back with regard to the GB squad and making hockey a real full-time career.'

On 25th November Cardiff Devils exact revenge for their Norwich Union loss as they defeat the Durham Wasps 10-0 at home in Wales. This is the first time in the league that Durham have failed to get on the scoreboard. This together with an 11-3 win at

Whitley Bay puts the Devils six points clear at the top.

The beginning of December sees the final of the Norwich Union Cup, between the Murrayfield Racers and the Durham Wasps played… at Basingstoke! The BIHA point out that the final is a show case for the sport and this together with the requirements of the BBC, who show the final on Grandstand, makes Basingstoke an ideal venue. Nearly half way through the first period Grandstand viewers see their first fight as Murrayfield's Chris Kelland and Durham's Rick Brebant are sent to the early shower. Yet again the fight gains more column inches than the game as journalists argue whether it is or isn't the worst thing to happen to the sport.

> Ian: *'There always is a load of debate. People worry that some viewers don't understand ice hockey and just see the fight.'*

> Stephen: *'I remember the game. It was a good game, I watched it on TV. I think Chris Kelland was injured and that's why he drew Rick into a fight. Obviously Rick was the top scorer for Durham so it was a good ploy by Murrayfield to get him out of the game.'*

Murrayfield Racers went on to win the game 10-4.

Rocky Saganiuk and Colin McHaffie have their bans resulting from the abandoned game in Whitley reduced on appeal.

In January with the deadline day fast approaching, several teams recruit new players. Nottingham replace defenceman Beaudoin with Keith Stewart and their season continues to improve. Other notable signings included the arrival of Keith Gretzky at Ayr in a blaze of publicity as the younger brother of the NHL's "Great One", Wayne Gretzky, came to Britain.

> Ian: *'It might have been a good PR stunt but he wasn't the success they hoped for.'*

Despite 2+2 on his home debut versus the Peterborough Pirates the Great One's brother hardly shone in his time at Ayr.

In Durham they sign Alexander Kozhevnikov, the first Soviet player to come to the UK. He had an outstanding career summary with two Olympic gold medals. Canadians tended to dominate the import positions in British Ice Hockey, though many clubs had tried out Europeans, like Nottingham this season, and many, like Nottingham's Beaudoin, had been replaced with a Canadian.

> Stephen: *'Especially at that time it was all small ice rinks and it was a known fact that the European Hockey players didn't like the physical contact. Its hard not to play physically in the small rinks. Now and in the next couple of years we're going to see more Europeans, because the ice surfaces are a lot bigger and the game is getting more technical. Plus Durham had a European coach at that time.'*

> Ian: *'And he was probably cheaper!'*

In Division One, January saw the demise of the Deeside Dragons, they fail to show up for a game in Humberside and are expelled two days later. Although their games are expunged from the league it made no impression on the league standings as poor Deeside had played and lost to every team in the league; eighteen games no points, 89 goals for and 316 against! Telford's Gerad Waslen is still Division One's top scorer despite losing 39 points when the Deeside Dragons records were deleted.

The beginning of February sees Tony Hand crash through the 100 point barrier for the sixth straight season. His team, Murrayfield Racers, are on a phenomenal winning streak setting a new single season record of 21 games without defeat. Despite this amazing run of form from the Scottish side, on the 4th March it is season long rivals from Wales who take their first Heineken Premier title as the Devils beat Peterborough at home.

Every year there is a special competition for the Scottish Teams. This year however there are only three possible entrants, Fife, Murrayfield and Ayr, so Cardiff are invited to join the competition. Held over the 10th and 11th of March Cardiff beat Ayr in the semi final whilst Murrayfield put out Fife. Once again it is Cardiff and Murrayfield battling for the honours. This time it is Murrayfield who take the spoils and win the Scottish Cup 13-4.

Heineken British League Premier Division	GP	W	L	D	GF	GA	Pts
Cardiff Devils	32	28	3	1	304	146	57
Murrayfield Racers	32	23	6	3	273	169	49
Durham Wasps	32	20	10	2	261	209	42
Solihull Barons	32	16	15	1	218	209	33
Fife Flyers	32	14	15	3	226	264	31
Nottingham Panthers	32	12	18	2	183	185	26
Ayr Raiders	32	9	19	4	181	229	22
Peterborough Pirates	32	7	25	0	174	281	14
Whitley Warriors	32	6	24	2	202	330	14

Tied teams are separated by the results between them.

Player of the Year (voted for by the British Ice Hockey Writers Association) and top scorer for the league this year was Cardiff Devils Steve Moria with 175 points from 30 games.

> Ian: *'Excellent player. For many of the years that he has been over here he's been one of the best if not the best player in the league, certainly the most talented. And back then he made it look so easy. Very good player to play with, having been on the same line as him.'*

From 20th to 25th March Great Britain competed in the World and European Championships Pool D, held this year in … Cardiff. Six dual national players join the GB squad including Cardiff's John Lawless and Chris Kelland of Murrayfield Racers. Only three teams take part, Great Britain, Spain and Australia. Each team plays the others twice.

First up for the GB squad is Australia. The first two periods go the way of the home team 5-0 and in the third they score another four to take the game 14-0. Apparently the score would have been much higher but for the heroics of Australian goalie Damian Holland. In goal for GB, Cardiff's Jeff Smith and Nottingham's David Graham share the duties. The last time these two teams met was in 1979 when GB won by a slightly narrower margin 5-3.

Next up for the Great Britain team is Spain. Stephen Johnson ensures GB were first to score but then the Spaniards equalise at 16.48 in the first period. Tony Hand regains the lead for Britain at 18.26 and from then on GB play with more purpose taking the second period 5-0 and the third 6-0 to win 13-1.

On March 24th GB play Australia again and secure promotion to Pool C with a 13-3 win. Finally Great Britain take on the Spaniards and win 17-3, despite the fact that GB struggle to motivate themselves with promotion already in the bag. Ian Cooper scores four goals which is the best one game tally of the Championship.

> Ian: 'That was a good tournament. Australia and Spain. It was mainly Cardiff supporters because we had five or six Cardiff players in the squad. It was good to win, no matter which Pool you're playing in, to get that promotion is great.'

The Australian goalie Damian Holland picked up the award for best netminder of the tournament whilst best defenceman went to British born and bred Stephen Cooper and best forward to Scottish born and bred Tony Hand.

Again this year the members of the GB team returned to their league teams to take part in the Play-Off Championships. Group A consisted of Solihull Barons, Nottingham Panthers and Cardiff Devils whilst in Group B Murrayfield Racers battled it out with local rivals Fife Flyers and the Durham Wasps. In the first games of the play-offs Nottingham Panthers held Cardiff to a six all draw, whilst Fife Flyers surprisingly thrashed the Wasps 13-3 at home. The next night it was Cardiff's turn as they thrashed Solihull 11-3, but the Wasps recovered well to tie 7-7 with Murrayfield back home at the Riverside rink.

The next weekend saw Cardiff and Nottingham secure their semi-final places at the expense of Solihull. Murrayfield had a firm grip of their group, which left Durham and Fife to fight it out for the last remaining spot. Durham made life difficult for themselves when they suspended Anthony and Stephen Johnson for the Murrayfield game after they apparently missed practice, and then the Racers managed to keep the high scoring Kozhevnikov off the score sheet and win the game. Then, against the odds, Fife turned over the Racers at Murrayfield in front of the BBC cameras and put an end to Durham's Wembley visits for the first time since 1985. This meant that when Fife and Durham met for the final game of the group at Durham on 15th April it was a bad tempered affair and Chief Referee, Nico Toeman, handed out a record 130 penalty minutes as Durham took the game 10-2.

The first semi-final is played on Friday 20th April between the Cardiff Devils and the Fife Flyers. This was the first time the tournament had been held over three days and it was mainly for the benefit of the BBC. Some fans had threatened to stay away but there were 8,537 in attendance for this game and 8,704 on Saturday for the second semi. Cardiff took on the Fife Flyers at 8:30pm on the Friday.

> Stephen: 'The team winning on Friday definitely had an advantage, more rest, more recovery, but we had earned that advantage - we were league champions and had come top of our play-off group. We'd earned our extra rest.
>
> The fans loved Wembley when it went to three days, it was normally over the Easter weekend so everyone could make the Friday as well. Fans would save up all year to make sure they had a good Wembley weekend and it was a great atmosphere.'

Stephen Cooper playing for Manchester Storm

Fife were the first to score as Paul Hand scored with just 25 seconds on the clock and Cardiff were unable to beat Craig Dickson in the Fife net until 18.25 to leave the first period tied at 1-1. The second period was goal less, but there were plenty of penalties as four from Fife and three from the Devils visit the penalty box. In the third period the Devils finally broke the dead lock when Steve Moria put the Devils in front after just two minutes. They then went on to score three more unanswered to take the first semi-final 5-1.

The second semi takes place at lunchtime on Saturday 21st between the Nottingham Panthers and the Murrayfield Racers. The Racers took the first period 2-1 and added another in the second period to make it 3-1 but the third saw Nottingham fight their way back scoring the first two goals to bring the game back. Then Murrayfield took the lead again. With just over two minutes left on the clock, Dampier pulled goalie David Graham in favour of another attacking player and Gavin Fraser tied the game. It looked as if the game would be heading for overtime when a long distance shot from Jim Mollard trickled across the line between David Graham's pads. Despite another six man attack from the Panthers the score remained and Murrayfield were through to the final.

British Junior C Championship
Wembley Arena 21st April

Nottingham Cougars 3   **Fife Flames...........1** (0-0, 3-0, 0-1)
Nottingham Scorers: Tait 2g, Trickett 1g, Richardson 1a, Bradbury 1a
Flames Scorers: King

The final faced off at 2pm on Sunday 22nd April. In charge was chief referee Nico Toeman with linesmen Gordon Pirry and Marcel Schuurkes. Despite losing the Scottish Cup to the Racers, Cardiff started as favourites and bookies William Hill made them 6-4 on. The Racers paid little attention to the odds and scored the first three goals of the first period. Ian Cooper was the first Devil on the score sheet at 17.51 and in the next two minutes Cardiff had pulled it back to three all for the end of the first period. The middle period saw only one goal, to put Murrayfield in the lead again 4-3. Murrayfield went on to make it 5-3 at the beginning of the third period but once again Ian Cooper began the fight back after 3.13 of the third period. There was a break in the play during the third period when a piece of the plexi glass had to be replaced and this gave Cardiff a chance to catch their breath as they iced fewer players during the game than Murrayfield. With less than two minutes on the clock Stephen Cooper scored the goal which brought the Devils level once again with the Racers and the game finished six all.

> Stephen: *'Quite emotional, a lot of pressure on us because we were behind the whole game, always fighting to come back. We'd score a goal and then they'd score another one. We kept catching up and then they'd pull away until the final ninety seconds when we equalised.'*

The game went into ten minutes sudden death overtime, but neither team could break the deadlock. So the penalties began. The first round saw five penalty shots taken by each team. For Cardiff Lawless, McEwen and Moria score whilst for Murrayfield so do Mollard, Kelland and McKee.

This takes the game into sudden death penalty shots. John Lawless is first to go again and then Scott Neil of Murrayfield scores. McEwen of Cardiff and Hand of Murrayfield both have shots saved. Moria and Mollard both score again. Next up Ian Cooper's shot is saved whilst Chris Kelland's shot hits the post. Stephen Cooper's shot is also saved but Brian McKee of Murrayfield misses. Lawless goes again but this time has his shot saved and Scott Neil misses. McEwen scores and then Tony Hand has his shot saved. Cardiff Devils win 6-5 on penalty shots.

> Ian: *'If you ask anyone about hockey who doesn't usually go to a match that is the one that they recall. Everyone can remember because it went on so long, it was on Grandstand so everyone got a chance to see it. The way it went into sudden death, and all the way through those rounds and rounds of penalty shots. It was huge, that was probably the backing of Heineken, for ten years they put millions into hockey and that attracted Grandstand. That's what makes sport big, the sponsorship and the TV coverage. Stephen scored the goal to take us into overtime and I passed it to him, but then we both missed penalty shots.'*

> Stephen: *'Great relief that the season was over and that we'd won the double. That was probably the best summer we ever had. People don't realise that to have a nice summer you need a successful season.'*

> Ian: *'Watching it on TV I remember I look really skinny, and Tony Hand missing his penalty shot.'*

> Stephen: *'He didn't miss it Jeff saved it'.*

> Ian: *'No, he just shot it into his body…'*

Coach of the Year for the Premier Division goes to Cardiff's coach Brian Kanewischer.

> Ian: *'Brian did an excellent job. He knew exactly what individuals he had on the team, how to treat them, what each guy needed for morale boosting and encouragement. He also knew what levels of coaching each guy required and which players he couldn't coach because he wasn't an in-depth technical type of guy. He worked hard, he got us working hard, he got everyone in the right frame of mind.'*

In the summer the Cooper brothers decide to return home to play for the Durham Wasps once more.

> Ian: *'We didn't have any problems in Cardiff, we were really happy but we were both still quite young. Durham, along with a sponsor they had, started a dialogue with me and Stephen and set up an attractive package, which we talked to Cardiff about and John Lawless eventually matched the offer. In the end it was purely a decision to go back home. Obviously Tom Smith had had to change his mind*

about paying British players. We were told that the set-up was different in Durham, the management was different and the players were treated better, and differently, and a promise of a new rink in two years. We signed a two year deal and we said if the ground hadn't been broken on the new rink at the end of those two years we would look to go elsewhere. Obviously we had two great years there, but there was no sign of the new rink and we moved back to Cardiff and settled straight back in.'

Season 1990/91
with
Rick Brebant
Canadian forward for the
Durham Wasps

	GP	G	A	PTS	PIM
Heineken Championship	8	18	34	52	16
Heineken League	35	93	116	209	72
Norwich Union Cup	11	24	44	68	32
Totals	54	135	194	329	120

HEINEKEN CHAMPIONS: Durham Wasps

PREMIER DIVISION: Durham Wasps

NORWICH UNION CUP: Durham Wasps

Chapter Three

Walking into Durham ice rink is something I will never forget. "Wow, what have I got myself into!" That's the first thing. I looked at the rink and I said, "I can't believe people play in a barn like this". No hot showers, one shower, if I remember correctly, that wasn't hot; we only trained two nights a week, Tuesday and Thursday, at like 9:30. But it gave me another opportunity. One of the reasons I came over was that I was allowed to have a job during the day, because most of the British guys did. It gave me an opportunity to further my career in terms of my education, so I dabbled in a few jobs and it was enjoyable. I was a car salesman for about 6 months; I worked at an antiques place which was really good, it was an antique auction house and I really enjoyed doing that, then for four years I was marketing manager for a construction firm. So I kept myself busy during the day. As the sport became more professional my working hours were cut back. When I was marketing manager as long as I had the job done, I might only put in thirty hours during the week, plus time I put in working at home, the people who ran the company were very good and understanding to my needs as a hockey player.'

Such were the thoughts of Rick Brebant as he looked back to his time as an import player at the infamous Durham Ice Rink, and the famous season 1990/91. Durham were the first British team Rick Brebant played for, he started his British Ice Hockey career with them in the 1987/88 season and continued to play for them until 1993.

Durham Ice Rink will forever be a part of the folklore of British Ice Hockey. It was opened in 1940, (the same year as the Nottingham Ice Stadium), by the famous 'Icy' Smith (twice Lord Mayor of Darlington) and remained largely untouched until its demise in 1996. In the 1940s there were 4,000 spectators every week for the ice hockey games. The building still stands as if nothing has changed but when you walk through those entrance doors now there is plush carpet and shiny new bowling alleys where once there were wooden stands and ancient ice. The Smith family owned the rink and ran the team for years. They lived in a house that was part of the rink with 'Icy' Smith's son Tom taking over and then his son Paul took over the running of the hockey team, whilst younger brother Damian was playing for the team. It was a family dynasty alongside a sporting one. For many years before the reformation of the British League the 'Icy' Smith Cup was recognised as the nearest thing to the British Championship.

In the summer of 1988 the Cooper brothers left Durham and signed for Cardiff, in the summer of 1989 the Johnson brothers left Durham and signed for Humberside. The home grown talent leaving Durham was having an adverse affect on the mighty Wasps, so in the summer of 1990 Durham bring back the Cooper brothers from Cardiff to their "home" rink.

'We went through turmoil the year before, not quite having the depth we needed and it was good to have the Coopers back. They are quality hockey players and they had proven themselves year in year out and to have them come back and get an import trio solidify really made our team have quite a bit of depth at that time. We had two solid lines, which was good in those days, and we could go into any game and we could be behind two or three goals and we knew we were going to win.'

31

The Norwich Union Cup began in September this year with all the Premier and Division One teams (except Glasgow) taking part. They were divided into four groups based on their league placings the previous year. Group A was topped by Cardiff Devils, Group B went to Murrayfield whilst Durham took Group C and Humberside Hawks were table toppers in Group D.

The beginning of October sees the start of the league campaign. It is not a good month for Czech players and coaches in the league. Fife had employed a Czech, Milan Figala, as coach after playing the 88-89 season for the Flyers. He employed two Czech players, but after failing to reach the semi finals of the Norwich Union Cup all three found themselves unemployed. Solihull Barons also found that the European style of their two Czech imports did not suit the bump and grind Canadian style usually found in British Ice Hockey, and released them. In Durham Czech coach George Peternousek resigns.

The semi-finals of the Norwich Union Cup were two legged home and away, played the last week of October and early in November, with Cardiff playing Durham; Wasps winning 15-8 on aggregate and Humberside taking on Murrayfield; Racers winning 16-11 on aggregate.

In Durham George Peternousek is replaced by John Page from the University of Victoria but he only lasted 48 hours in the Durham hot seat.

> *'I remember that, the first day he kinda came in and he gave us this big manual to read and know the plays by the next day. Then he bought sixteen used tyres'*

Rick laughs loudly.

> *'I remember that, sixteen used tyres that we were supposed to practice our powerplay with. He positioned them on the ice and we had to pass in and out. He had some wild ambitions; he never really treated the players as professionals. You know a University level player is a little bit different than a professional and in the end it cost him his job. We really never got to know how good a coach he was or how bad he was. I am glad that he didn't stay.'*

Murrayfield Racers were beaten 5-8 at home to Durham Wasps in October, their first home defeat for 364 days since 29th October 1989. Things got no better in November at Durham when the Wasps beat them 13-4, the Racers' heaviest loss for three years. Then on the 15th December at Whitley Bay the two teams meet again for the final of the Norwich Union Cup. *The Ice Hockey Annual* reports:

> *"Smiths' Revenge, the wags called it, as the sixth Norwich Union Cup final was played in the Far North, at Whitley Bay, after 1989s' Deep South game in Basingstoke. More importantly for Durhams' President Tom, his Wasps got their revenge on the ice as Racers relinquished the cup surprisingly easily.*

> *A final featuring these teams yet again was a tribute to their firm grip on this ever-growing sport....*

But the biggest disappointment of the 1990 Cup was the absence of BBC television at the final for the first time in Norwich Unions six season of sponsorship. No reason was given and the hoped for satellite TV coverage did not materialise. Oh well at least the final kept Tom Smith happy."

On December 22nd Durham's bogey team, Nottingham Panthers, thrash them 10-2: their first loss in thirteen games. Import Jason Hannigan played well for the Wasps but when his league form dipped towards the end of the year he was gone, replaced by Lloyd McKinnie who played four games before himself being replaced by Mike Blaisdell.

'Lloyd Mckinnie played two or three weeks. A really small forward, his size didn't go very well in our league. We had Jason who started off tremendously then he had a few problems late in the year, and then we got Mike and once he arrived it made everything all come together. I had a good year and a half with Mike. He's a tremendous hockey player and I thoroughly enjoyed playing with him.'

At the beginning of January Murrayfield go top of the league with a win at Cardiff 7-2, the first team to win there since Solihull on the 2nd December. This is also the first televised game of the season on BBC Grandstand's 'Game of the Month.' On January 13th Mike Blaisdell played his first game for the Wasps at Murrayfield and scores twice in their 9-3 win, taking Durham top of the league.

Blackburn Arena, with a capacity of 3,500, opened on 25th January and staged its first ice hockey the next day as the Blackburn Blackhawks took on Oxford City in front of a 1,500 crowd. The first goal was scored by Blackhawks Fred Perlini and the Blackhawks went on to take the game 6-3. The Blackhawks went on to finish the season in 4th place in the English League.

On February 2nd Cardiff Devils become only the second team to beat the Wasps. On the 7th Murrayfield part company with imported coach, Archie Henderson: the fourth imported coach to leave a Premier club so far this season.

'At that time they thought import coaches were the way to go plus I don't think there were many British coaches that had played the game at the highest level that could move in to coaching.'

The clubs wanted to progress and get away from the player coach but were not quite ready for the full import coach.

At the end of February Grant Slater, a British player for the Peterborough Pirates, is banned for the rest of the season for swinging his stick at two Ayr players, whilst at the beginning of March, Rick Fera is suspended for assaulting an official. March became an unpleasant month for the sport as Chelmsford Chieftain's imports refuse to play after Mike Urquhart is sent off at Haringey; and Solihull Barons share 101 penalty minutes with Peterborough Pirates. The Barons' Ron Shudra benches himself and other senior players in protest. Solihull's Brent Sapergia who received a game and gross misconduct is fined £250 and banned for three games and Shudra is fined £500. Haringey win 8-1 over the Chieftains and needless to say, the Pirates win against the 'junior' Barons (17-2).

Young British Player of the Year: Nicky Chinn of Cardiff Devils

Rick Brebant on Nicky Chinn:
'Nicky Chinn didn't start skating until he was seventeen. He is just one natural player that had good balance and good co-ordination. He was a big strong boy and he is even bigger and stronger now and he just had that natural ability and that little bit of cockiness that you need to be a good hockey player. He was well deserved of the award and he was one of the new breed of British player. You had him, Iain Robertson, Lobby [David Longstaff], Paul Dixon. We had the Coopers, Tony Hand and Scott Neil starting the British players off and showing them what they could achieve and these young people were the next wave. [At Calgary] You are playing with some pretty good hockey players and it is a good level monitor, to know where you have to go and where've you gone. It's a great experience - probably one that they should never forget, you know they haven't because they still talk about it. They got offers, they should have gone over there, got a couple of years coaching, if they had the opportunity; they could always come back here. It's a shame that they didn't. Visit another country for free, that's what its about, what more can you ask for?!!'

'They were trying to take the ugly side out of it. There was a time when a lot of coaches had younger British players that you sent out at the imports and try to get the imports off. You couldn't fight or you got chucked out of the game, and the imports couldn't afford to fight because if you are chucked out of the game you're going to hurt your team. In the end a lot of stick swinging incidents and bad elbows became part of the game because that's the only way the imports could protect themselves to a certain degree. I'm not saying all imports did it but you know they were sending out young kids that weren't a total asset to the club, like an import was, trying to get the imports out of the game and those times are very tough, to suck up to a stick, a spear, and things like that when the referees weren't calling it at that time.'

'You can't put it all on either the referees or sending the British players out to get the imports out: some of it was the control of the imports; probably not used to the standard of refereeing as the refereeing wasn't up to the standard of the play. When you are talking about ten teams, that's maybe two decent referees to cover five games and the standard was poor and it frustrated a lot of imports and at times they really lashed out, which wasn't good for the game. On the other hand, to bench yourselves was not good for the game either, the people who suffer are not only the team, but also the fans, and the fans pay to see you play and they expect you to give 100% no matter what's going on, on the ice. It's your job, and they're basically paying your wages. It was a shame, but I think the sport has moved on leaps and bounds since then and hopefully it will continue to do so.'

Durham Wasps clinch the league title and their second piece of silverware on March 2nd with a win over struggling Fife Flyers.

Rick Brebant as player coach of the Durham Wasps (1996/96)

Rick Brebant finished top of the scoring chart with 93 goals and 209 points, Claude Dumas of Whitley Warriors was second having scored more goals than Rick (101) but collected fewer assists, giving him a total of 185 points. Top of the netminding averages was Durham's goalie Chris Salem with a goals against average of 5.23, second is David Graham of Nottingham with 5.34.

From March 23rd to April 3rd, Britain were in action in Pool C of the World & European Championships in Copenhagen, Denmark.

Heineken British League Premier Division	GP	W	L	D	GF	GA	Pts
Durham Wasps	36	28	5	3	324	186	59
Cardiff Devils	36	21	13	2	274	237	44
Peterborough Pirates	36	19	13	4	287	241	42
Murrayfield Racers	36	19	15	2	264	236	40
Ayr Raiders	36	18	15	3	243	243	39
Nottingham Panthers	36	16	16	4	200	202	36
Whitley Warriors	36	13	19	4	269	292	30
Solihull Barons	36	13	22	1	255	340	27
Cleveland Bombers	36	9	22	5	198	246	23
Fife Flyers	36	8	24	4	215	306	20

This year was to see four teams, instead of the usual one or two, promoted from Pool C and hopes were high for the British team. There were six dual national, or British-Canadian players on the team including Chris Kelland who was also Captain.

The first game was against the Chinese, and despite out shooting the opposition in both the second and third periods, GB lost five goals to six. The second game saw a 7-2 win over North Korea, Tony Hand scoring a hat trick in the first half of the game. Denmark were the next opponents and the scores were level until six seconds from the final hooter when Denmark put the winner past 'Bernie' McCrone to take the game 3-2.

Moray Hanson had been between the pipes for the first game, John 'Bernie' McCrone was in fine form for the next two games in the GB goal, and for the next game coach Alex Dampier put his third goalie in the net, David Graham. David got a shut-out with GB winning 11-0 over Belgium, which took them to joint fourth in the table with Hungary, who were the next team the British were to face.

'Bernie' McCrone was back on netminding duties for the game with Hungary, but it was a lack of shots on goal and too many trips to the penalty box which put paid to GB's chances of winning this game, and it finished three all. The next game against the Bulgarians was a similar story with GB going from 0-2 down to 4-2 up during one twelve minute period, but too many trips to the penalty box was enough to let the Bulgarians back in and win 5-4. The South Koreans scored on their first shot in the next game but that was their first and last as GB went on to win 7-1.

The last game of the Championship for the British was against Romania, one of the stronger hockey nations. This was one of the best performances from the GB side. The first period was tied 2-2, then the British team takes the second period 3-0 for a 5-2 lead, then the Romanians came back to 5-4 before both teams scored in the last two minutes, for GB to take the game 6-5. Chris Kelland who did not play in the last game due to an injury, was voted tournament's best defenceman but GB had failed to make the all-important fourth placed finish.

World & European Championship: Pool C	GP	W	L	D	GF	GA	Pts
Denmark	8	7	0	1	71	13	15
China	8	6	1	1	44	24	13
Romania	8	6	2	0	51	22	12
Bulgaria	8	4	3	1	35	26	9
Great Britain	8	4	3	1	45	25	9
Hungary	8	3	4	1	37	32	7
North Korea	8	2	5	1	29	35	5
South Korea	8	1	7	0	19	64	2
Belgium	8	0	8	0	11	101	0

On the resumption of the British season the BIHA allowed Murrayfield to replace injured Chris Kelland with Basingstoke's Mike Rowe for the first two weeks of the play-offs because Kelland was injured whilst on GB duty. Peterborough started the campaign with a surprise 9-7 defeat of the Grand Slam seeking Durham Wasps, whilst Whitley Warriors were beating Championship holders Cardiff Devils.

Then Durham were involved in the continuing Brent Sapergia saga. After scoring a hat-trick against Ayr, Brent was chucked out of the game. Then the Wasps game with Solihull was abandoned with 1.04 still on the clock, referee Ken Taggart had handed out 386 penalty minutes (Pims). When the teams met again Sapergia was sent off for attacking Stephen Cooper. A total of five players were suspended by the Disciplinary Committee.

> *'We had a few rows with Solihull, especially in the play-offs. We met them away first and there was a big brawl and the game was suspended with minutes left. The next game was back at our rink and this guy is a little bit of a nut case and he had things to prove and he came out and he skated across the ice and tried to cross-check but Stephen ducked! He was thrown out of the game - he wasn't very good for the game. He was a gifted, hard working, sharp player, but as they say, he had the tools but no tool box. Over here at that time, imports could not afford to be sitting in the box, eight, ten or twelve minutes a game because you were required on the ice. He never really adjusted to the game in this country.'*

Durham Ice Rink

Despite the suspensions Durham, went on to top Group A and go through with Peterborough Pirates, whilst in Group B, Cardiff Devils led the pack with Murrayfield taking second spot, still icing Mike Rowe as Chris Kelland was still not fit to play.

This year's Wembley finals were played over three days with the first semi final on Friday 26th April at 8pm between the Cardiff Devils and Peterborough Pirates with

8,467 fans in attendance. Inspired by Rocky Saganiuk, the Pirates were hungrier for the win than the defending champions, Devils were not led until 48.35 when Danny Shea, who had been in the Ayr team that Rocky coached to Wembley two years previously, scored the third Pirates goal in less than three minutes. The Pirates went on to win 7-4 with the Devils unable to get enough shots past a hot Scott O'Connor playing in the Peterborough net.

The second semi was played on Saturday 27th at 1pm between the Durham Wasps and the Murrayfield Racers. Again there was a game changing three goals, this time in under two minutes at the beginning of the third period, changing a Racers lead 6-4 to a Durham lead 7-6. Durham went on to score four more unanswered goals taking the final score to 11-6.

'That was a pretty good game. We were behind going into the third period and then we came back with a really strong third and ended up clinching it.'

British Junior C Championship
Wembley Arena 27th April

Fife Flames...........5   Romford Hornets 0 (1-0, 2-0, 2-0)
Flames Scorers: King 2+1, Grubb 2g, Renton 1g, Simpson, Dingwall, Lynch 1a

---

Then the Final was played on Sunday April 28th at 2pm. Chief Stripey Nico Toeman was in charge with Simon Kirkham and Alan Craig the linesmen. The start of the game was delayed by 30 minutes because the Wasps kit was found to have been trashed in their Wembley changing room.

'Oh yes, some people got in to the dressing room and kinda urinated and put excrement on various pieces of equipment belonging to our team. It was pretty disgusting, and dulled a few skates and various things like that. That was weird, we had a cocky team at that time, it had to be pretty cocky - we knew how good we were and we were confident. We had won the Norwich Union, we'd won the league and no-one wanted us to win the Grand Slam. It was one of those things that people would do whatever they wanted to do to try and stop us.'

Rick had a clear idea in his own mind who had been the perpetrators but there was no investigation and no action was taken. Having made it through the semis, Durham had Anthony Payne and Damian Smith fresh and ready to play in the final having returned from the suspensions handed out after the Solihull game. Once the game began Durham was never in danger, winning the first period 2-1, the second 3-1 and tying the third for a final score of 7-4 to take both the Championship and also the Grand Slam. Local heroes Anthony Payne and Ivor Bennett had a big impact and Ivor Bennett picked up the Man of the Match award for Durham.

'We knew going in to the final, because a couple of players didn't play the night before, because they were suspended, we knew that if we got through the semi

final, which was very difficult, that we needed these guys and to have them back in the line-up with fresh legs really meant a lot. If I remember correctly they had a tremendous game and scored a couple of big goals for us. In the end the first lines cancelled themselves out and it came down to our second line doing the business. That's part of the team effort - they were fresh, full of pizzazz. It was good for Ivor, because that was towards the end of his career, to win Man of the Match. I think he got a goal and an assist, he played really well.'

Durham Wasps were only the second team to take the Grand Slam (first were Dundee Rockets in 83/84) and it was a record third Championship for them. Peterborough Pirates were coached to third in the league and runners up in the Championship by Rocky Saganiuk. Rocky had achieved similar success at Wembley with Ayr Bruins two years previously. Peterborough also made it the first all English final in their Wembley debut. Rocky was rewarded with the accolade of Coach of the Year for the Premiership.

'I have a lot of admiration for Rocky. He brought a team that was probably average in talent and made them play out of their skin. They peaked at the right time in the play-offs - he had them full of enthusiasm he had them really, really going for it. They deserved to be in the final and they were going to be a really tough team to beat, because one-off games you can play with a lot of emotion and really get in to it. He had the ability to get the players really psyched up and ready and they would go through a wall for him and that's what they did and it was a good final.'

Rick Brebant was awarded Player of the Year whilst team mate Stephen Cooper as well as picking up the Alan Weeks Trophy for best British Defenceman also took Players' Player of the Year.

'He was head and shoulders above the rest, there was nothing more. At that time he was probably one of the top three defencemen whether they were imports or not. If you had the Cooper brothers it was like another two imports. They knew the game, they knew how to play and they came to play and were really good professionals. They brought it to another level; they kinda opened the doors to show what the British players can achieve. They were the pioneers to British players by making hockey a way of living. And through their professional attitude, their commitment to the game and their ability on the ice, you know they, along with Tony Hand, were pioneers for the British game and where its gone since then.'

In May the BIHA suspended Brent Sapergia until December 31st 1991 and told Solihull they could only play with two imports for the first six games of the next season. Brent had not limited his activities to game time and had also been arrested in February after a disturbance at a Birmingham nightclub and released on bail. When he left the country in April to return to the USA it was unlikely that Britain would see Brent Sapergia again.

In the promotion/relegation play-offs the top six Division One teams and the bottom two teams from the Premiership were divided into two groups with the winner of each gaining a Premiership spot next season. Group A contained last year's promoted team, Cleveland Bombers, but they lost their slot with Bracknell Bees topping the group. In

Group B the once mighty Fife Flyers were pushed to third in the group, making way for the stars of the Division One season Humberside Seahawks to be promoted to the top flight. The Seahawks had only lost four games all season whilst Fife had undergone a season of turmoil with four different coaches and ten different imports. The gloom over Fife was only lifted by the shining light of Iain Robertson, last year's Young British Player of the Year, in his play for Fife and the British team at the World Championships and the emphatic win by the Fife Flames in the junior final at Wembley.

SEASON 1991/92

WITH

'ROCKET' RON SHUDRA

CANADIAN DEFENCEMAN FOR THE
SHEFFIELD STEELERS

	GP	G	A	PTS	PIM
ENGLISH LEAGUE	32	78	70	148	42
PROMOTION PLAY-OFFS	6	15	14	29	4
TOTALS	**38**	**93**	**84**	**177**	**46**

HEINEKEN CHAMPIONS: DURHAM WASPS

PREMIER DIVISION: DURHAM WASPS

AUTUMN CUP: NOTTINGHAM PANTHER

Chapter Four

The beginning of the 91/92 season started on the last day of August with eleven Autumn Cup games attracting some 20,000 fans, some of whom saw relegated Fife beat the Grand Slam Champions Durham Wasps 11-5. The season began fairly normally for the fans of Solihull. Captain Ron Shudra was forced to serve the remainder of Brent Sapergias' ban. Dave Simms had signed import goalie Wayne Cowley and he was soon the fans' favourite. However, off the ice things were looking bad for the team and the BIHA asked the club to post a bond of £60,000 with them to ensure the team's financial ability to make it through the season. Solihull cannot find the money and suddenly David Gardner-Brown announces a rescue package for the Solihull club, which means moving the whole lot to the Sheffield Arena. The Sheffield Arena was built as part of the facilities for the World Student Games and was opened by the Queen in May 1991. The state of the art building has a capacity for ice hockey of 8,500. Sheffield was already home to the Sheffield Sabres ice hockey team at the old Mecca Ice Rink on Queens Road, but in comparison the spectator capacity was a mere 500.

The BIHA decided that Gardner-Brown's rescue package was not the way forward, so Gardner-Brown failed in his bid to buy a ready made team and Solihull drop out of the Premier to compete in the ED1(English Division 1). The new Sheffield team would also start their life in ED1, if Gardner-Brown could get a team together. Relegated Cleveland Bombers, now known as Billingham Bombers, gain a reprieve and replace Solihull in the Premier League fixtures. Ron Shundra recalls:

'When we went into the season we [Solihull] were fine. We played the last Cup games because we were there and they needed a home gate so we let them get the home gate to try and pay the guys.'

'I waited until the end of the trophy and then got in touch with Basingstoke and trained down there for a week or so. By then Ronnie Wood knew he was coming up here [to Sheffield]. They offered me a contract down there, Ronnie said "don't sign anything - come up here first", so I came up, saw the building said "yeh sure we'll try it, go from there." For the first three weeks me and Ronnie were travelling up from Birmingham everyday, early mornings and late nights!'

The only Steelers game that Ron Shudra didn't play in that first season was a challenge match between Durham Wasps and a Sheffield Select side coached by Tom Smith of Durham on Thursday September 26th. The Sheffield side consisted mainly of loaned Humberside players as the collapse of the Solihull deal left Gardner-Brown without a team to ice. The first goal went to the new team but was scored by Humberside's Anthony Johnson assisted by his brother Stephen. Durham went on to score seven unanswered goals. The official attendance was given as 2,300 but it seemed a lot less in a building designed for 8,000.

Ron Shudra's first game for the Sheffield Steelers was the first of their English League Division campaign which was hosted by Sunderland.

'Our first game was in Sunderland and I think we had only practised once.'

Despite their lack of preparation, Steelers went on to win 13-2. The next night was their first league game at home to Chelmsford. 'Magic' Mark Mackie scored the first goal of the night at 8.41 then the teams went on to draw three all. The crowd was a disappointing 300 but the priority in the preceding couple of weeks was to sign a team to meet the league fixtures, the crowd would come later.

'It was very empty but it was the week after I signed. We didn't have time to do anything so it was basically all the people from the old Queens Road.'

In the Autumn Cup, the preliminary round was divided into three groups. Durham Wasps top Group A and go on to play Humberside who were the runners up with the most points from the three groups. Nottingham topped Group B and went on to play the Cardiff Devils from the top of Group C.

Nottingham won the double headed semi 13-10 on aggregate whilst last year's Grand Slammer's, Durham Wasps, were put out of this year's Autumn Cup by the narrowest of margins 15-14 to Humberside in the fourth minute of overtime after 120 minutes had failed to divide them.

October was a good month for Humberside who also chalked up the first Premier white wash in four years when they shut out Billingham Bombers 6-0 at home.

In November the Sheffield Steelers secure the services of forward Steve Nemeth, veteran of 12 NHL games with the New York Rangers.

'We only had six or seven core guys out of the nineteen guys, not saying anything bad about the others, we were just still trying to find players, but we were always looking for imports. When his name came up [Steve Nemeth] I said "I've played a few games with him and against him and he is a good skater and he should be able to score a few goals."'

On November 17th in their sixth home game of the season, Steelers shut out Sunderland 14-0 with local player Andy Havenhand between the pipes.

'Andy was our goalie, he was the one. He was another one that was never taught anything, how to play goal, how to do angles, it doesn't take much if guys are willing to listen and learn. He came out and I said a few things because I had seen goalie coaches in Canada. I just took some drills that they did and transferred them over to Andy and he worked very hard and it paid off. He was a good goalie for us.'

The Steelers achieved a new record that night too, this time they attracted 5,527 fans to the game, the biggest crowd for a league match since the first British League folded 31 years ago. At that stage the Steelers were working hard to attract an audience to the game.

'We went pretty much anywhere with tickets, any football club, womens dinner, any chance to get any exposure.'

The inside of Sheffield Arena

But whilst Sheffield were heralded as the next cheque book hockey club - the first to go fully professional – the reality at that time was far from it, with most of the British guys working their day jobs like any of the other clubs. More practice sessions from this new professional team?

'The funny thing about it, in Solihull we were Tuesday/Thursday night ten till twelve, and then play the weekend. The first year we were here, I think we only practised six times, whenever there was ice in the arena that's when we practised. We didn't practice at Queens Road ever. So basically the day before the game and maybe we would skate on game day. So we went from two practices a week to almost no practices a week and you could see it in the games.'

The imports were working as hard in the office as on the ice.

'We were in the office, Steve and I, all year. We were in the back doing whatever we were doing, shaking hands, kissing babies, or in the office talking to people, visiting companies trying to get sponsorship, phone calls, letters, merchandise. The next year was a little better because we started practising in the arena and at Queens Road a little.'

Being an import on the ice for any British team was hard work, as David Graham and Rick Brebant have described. Most clocked up 50+ minutes a game and it was no different in ED1 for the Steelers' imports.

'Choose your spot to take a penalty. What situation can you afford to take a penalty, when you are really tired, take a tripping penalty, make sure it was a good one make sure the guy's got an obvious chance. Stay away from the rough stuff if you could, because you couldn't afford to be taken out. A lot of the British guys would come up against the imports to try and take them out, and you had to take it and skate away from it. And you had to do it, you had to do it, and then sooner or later you'd snap and you'd give it right back to them and of course they'd done their job, you are off the ice for the penalty. So you had to be a smart player as well as a point scorer and leader.'

In the Heineken league Ron could see the gradual improvement year on year.

' The game was evolving a little, the players were getting better, and getting better guys brought in, and coaching was getting a little better, so the game improves and defensively everything has got better to where we are now.'

Young British Player of the Year: Paul Dixon of Humberside Hawks

Ron Shudra on Paul Dixon:
'He was here the next season. Good young player, he worked really hard when he was here. Smart guy, still playing now, one of the better defencemen, other than Cooper, maybe better than Stephen now, I think. Attitude-wise always wanted to play, always had a good heart for the game, good instinct for the game. It was good experience to go out and see what they measured up against if they took it to go over there and to learn something not just to go over and "be there", and I think Paul went and learned some stuff.'

November saw the mighty Durham Wasps suffer their longest losing run for eight years when they went four without a win but they put it right on the 16th beating Ayr 9-4. Shannon Hope of the Cardiff Devils is disciplined for fighting with Chris Kelland, now of Nottingham Panthers, during the post game handshake. His ban of eleven games is later reduced to six games. On the weekend of the 23rd/24th November a festival of hockey, as Sheffield Arena play host to the Autumn Cup and, Autumn Trophy finals. In the cup Nottingham Panthers started with a 3-0 first period against Humberside Hawks. Hawks brought it back to 4-4 in the second before Nottingham went ahead again to run out 7-5 winners. This was Nottingham's first trophy since Wembley '89. All the English League teams (except Sheffield and Solent whose Arenas were not ready in time for the start of the competition) and those Heineken teams not involved in the cup, took part in the Autumn Trophy. The finalists were Swindon Wildcats and Milton Keynes Kings who could not be separated in either sixty minutes or after another 10 minutes of overtime, the scores were still level at five all. The trophy finally went to Swindon 3-2 on penalty shots.

In the beginning of December the Premier sees only one point between the top four sides, with recently promoted Humberside topping the table and Nottingham, Durham and Cardiff snapping at their heels. Then on 22nd Durham shut-out the Bracknell Bees 15-0 to take the top of the table.

December proved to be a critical month for the Steelers too. On the 22nd they played Streatham and the game proved to be a turning point as far as the crowd was concerned. It was a tight game from the beginning but at one point in the second period the Steelers were up 6-4 but back came Streatham. Sheffield were losing going in to the last two minutes of the game. Some of the fans started to leave, but what they missed was an amazing come back performance with three goals - 'Magic' Mark Mackie living up to his name (58.15 &58.44) and then 'Rocket' Ron Shudra put away the game winner at 59.41. Slightly different from the game the night before when the Steelers had entertained Sunderland Chiefs and beaten them 29 goals to four. But the crowd had been bitten with hockey fever watching the Sunday night Streatham game and word of what was happening down at the Arena started to spread.

'We were up to 4,000 or so, but we were still giving away tickets, and then after that game where we were two goals down and we came back in the last minute and half to win. From then on it started picking up and picking up. That was the key turning point right there. That game, the result, and the word got around.'

Approaching Christmas Sheffield are in second place, having played less games than league leaders Medway Bears.

English League First Division	GP	W	L	D	GF	GA	Pts
Medway Bears	15	12	2	1	186	52	25
Sheffield Steelers	13	11	1	1	134	70	23
Streatham Redskins	15	9	6	0	149	116	18
Oxford City Stars	13	8	4	1	131	82	17
Chelmsford Chieftans	15	6	8	1	116	137	13
Solent Vikings	17	6	11	0	166	224	12
Haringey Racers	14	5	9	0	88	121	10
Solihull Barons	15	5	10	0	104	146	10
Sunderland Chiefs	15	2	13	0	88	214	4

On December 28th the first home international for seven years, Scotland versus England, is played in front of the TV cameras. These fixtures had been played 48 times at irregular intervals since 1909, England have won 19 and three have been drawn. The match was revived by the BIHA as a showcase event for television and to help fund-raising for the British team in the World Championships. Although there was some controversy over dual nationals, Scotland didn't want to ice any but were persuaded to use two by the BIHA. It was deemed to be a triumph for the sport with 3,000 watching at Murrayfield and many more on television.

In January the impact of Sheffield's Streatham game kicks in for their game on the 18th 6,000 tickets are sold by Tuesday, 7,300 by Friday the remaining tickets are gone, four hours before face off. 8,300 tickets sold, no hand outs. Despite losing this one to close rivals the Medway Bears 7-9 the second full house occurs on February 1st and they witness a 16-3 win over Solent Vikings.

'Plan to actual numbers was night and day, we never expected anything like that, getting the people coming in, that was demand, there was that much demand for tickets. The way it went on a scale was just straight up after Christmas, no-one predicted that, no-one expected that.'

Ron Shudra in Steelers Uniform

At the end of January the Heineken awards go to Paul Smith of Durham for coach of the month, Durham's Rick Brebant for highest point scorer and Chris Salem, Durham's goalie, for a shut-out. This is exactly the same as the previous month's awards, the first time this had happened in the nine seasons of Heineken hockey action.

Durham clinch their fifth league title on February 23rd at Ayr but the weekend news is of a nasty incident in Bracknell the night before. In a feisty game that saw three players ejected in the first period, later in the game Lee Odelein of Bracknell was hit by seventeen stone Roger Hunt of Murrayfield, during a break in the play. Odelein was hospitalised with a broken jaw, fractured cheekbone and concussion.* Hunt is questioned by the police after the game and later charged. This incident got more column inches in the papers than anything that happened during the playing of the game this season. The

BIHA later issue life bans on both Hunt and Murrayfield's coach Leo Koopmans, who sent Hunt out during the stoppage. Whilst condemning the injuries inflicted on Odelien, some hockey press point out, as have many of the players that have contributed to the book, that it was not unusual for coaches to send players out to 'disrupt' the imports and try and get them out of the game. The unfortunate thing in this case was that Roger Hunt saw an opportunity during the break in play to take this import "out of the game" and he took his opportunity before thinking through the possible consequences of his actions. The life ban and charging by the police must have given both Hunt and others involved in hockey plenty to think about.

In the last game of the month Durham lose their unbeaten run, tripped up again by the Nottingham Panthers 7-6 in Nottingham, but the league title was already in the bag.

> 'They were a very good club. In their little building they wouldn't lose, you'd go in knowing you had lost before you went in there. That's the way it was because everything seemed to go against you in that building whether it was the boards, the clock, the refs everything seemed to go their way. Nothing you did seemed to get you a result. That was one key thing that they did; they were very, very solid at home and on the road they did what they had to do to win no matter what it was, and that's how you get a winning streak. Twenty-seven games is phenomenal, they had a very good club.'

In Sheffield an extra 1,200 seats are installed and filled for the final two games of the season on 14th/15th March. The Saturday crowd rebreaks the Steelers own record for the modern era and with 9,750 comes close to breaking the all time British record for an ice hockey game, though no-one is too sure what that figure is!

From 18-24th March Pool C of the World Championships came to the Hull Ice Arena in Britain. The previous year had seen four teams promoted out of Pool C, so hopes were high for the GB squad this year. It was important too to do well this year as the break up of the Soviet Union had led to many of the countries from the old USSR applying to join the tournament in their own right for next year and they would join in Pool C.

This year's GB team included eight dual nationals. New to the team were Durham's defenceman Mike O'Connor, Shannon Hope of Cardiff and Kevin Conway of Basingstoke. New British trained players included netminder Scott O'Connor from Peterborough, Shaun Johnson of Humberside who joined his two brothers who had been capped before and Damian Smith of Durham. Their first game was against Australia. GB outshot the Aussies 72-12 and took the game 10-2. Scott O'Connor replaced McCrone in the nets at 30.21 after the chance of a shut-out was gone but with GB enjoying total domination of the play.

In their next game it was Scott O'Connor who started in the nets and Tony Hand led the way against South Korea, putting the first past them with only 69 seconds on the clock. Great Britain went on to gain the shut-out with a final score of 15-0. GB found

---

* Hunt later returned to this country, paid a fine and went to be player/coach for Murrayfield Royals. (See chapter eight).

themselves a goal down for the first time in the tournament after four minutes of the game against Belgium, and for a while looked a little edgy until 12.38 when John Iredale of Whitley hit the roof of the net to equalise. GB went on to win 7-3. The attendance of 948 was the lowest of all of the GB games.

Game twelve of the tournament saw Great Britain take on the North Koreans in front of 1768 fans. The Danish referee dismissed two British players for retaliation in the first period, but this did not stop Tony Hand scoring the first goal at 4.01. He went on to score a short handed goal which began as GB were killing a five on three penalty. Tony Hand gained possession of the puck, maintained possession as he circled the defensive zone, passed to Stephen Cooper at the blueline before skating up the ice for the return pass (at which point GB had one man returned to the ice) Hand then went one-on-one with the Korean netminder and beat him for the goal of the tournament. Alex Dampier said after the game, " The Tony Hand Roadshow. He did a hell of a job, taking the puck end-to-end and showing why he is one of the best kids in the country."

For their last game of the tournament GB took on the Hungarians in front of some 1812 fans. Before the tournament began this game had been marked down as the tournament decider but the Hungarians had lost to North Korea and Australia, so GB had already clinched the gold medal and promotion to Pool B. The game was relaxed, with GB only taking four penalty minutes (compared to 47 in the North Korea game and 31 in the Begium game). GB took the first period 3-0 the second 6-0 before easing up in the third allowing the Hungarians to score three for a 5-3 third period and a 14-3 game.

World Championship: Pool C	GP	W	L	D	GF	GA	Pts
Great Britain	5	5	0	0	62	10	10
North Korea	5	2	2	0	25	28	6
Australia	5	2	2	1	24	26	5
Hungary	5	2	3	0	18	33	4
Belgium	5	2	3	0	17	24	4
South Korea	5	0	4	1	18	43	1

So for next year the Great Britain team would be playing in Pool B of the World Championships. Coach Alex Dampier, speaking to *Ice Hockey News Review*, was quick to point out that to repeat such success would be highly unlikely.

> *"Its right back to square one. We're a little higher up the totem pole, but we are at the bottom again. Basically it will be back to survival. We want to stay in Pool B and we want to make sure that people know we are there."*

The top eight teams in the Premier league qualified for the championship play-offs. They were divided into two groups with the league leaders going into Group A and the runners up into Group B, the rest of the groups were decided by a draw. The final standings in the league:

Heineken British League Premier Division	GP	W	L	D	GF	GA	Pts
Durham Wasps	36	26	4	6	314	162	58
Nottingham Panthers	36	21	12	3	238	192	45
Cardiff Devils	36	20	13	3	235	204	43
Humberside Seahawks	36	18	13	5	224	203	41
Murrayfield Racers	36	18	16	2	234	218	38
Whitley Warriors	36	16	17	3	250	246	35
Norwich & P'boro Pirates	36	13	15	8	201	225	34
Billingham Bombers	36	11	20	5	184	258	27
Bracknell Bees	36	9	25	2	167	264	20
Ayr Raiders	36	8	25	3	176	251	19

So Group A consisted of the mighty Durham Wasps, Norwich & Peterborough Pirates, Murrayfield Racers, and Humberside Seahawks. Group B had Nottingham Panthers, Whitley Warriors, Cardiff Devils, and Billingham Bombers. The first weekend saw the Cardiff Devils jinxed by the BBC TV cameras, or so the excuse goes, being beaten at home by the Panthers 5-7. Surprisingly Durham are held to a five all draw with Humberside whilst Peterborough hold Murrayfield to the same score. In that game Murrayfield's Tony Hand fractured his wrist but only missed one game and returned to score 5 goals and 8 assists -13 points in his next three outings. Despite his valiant efforts, Murrayfield are put out in a bad tempered TV clash at home to Durham. The last game between Whitley and Cardiff is a thriller which finished 8-4 to the Warriors and sees them into the semi-finals.

The first semi-final was contested between Nottingham Panthers and Norwich & Peterborough Pirates coached by that man Rocky Saganuick again, on Friday 24th April. The first period sees the first ever scoreless opening period at Wembley but in the second six are scored leaving the teams now tied on three. In the final period Nottingham scored four unanswered after Dan Dorion's third goal went in from behind the net off the Pirates' goalie's skate wrecking his confidence and opening the floodgates.

The second semi-final played on Saturday 25th April sees Durham Wasps take on local rivals Whitley Warriors. Although Durham had a two goal lead at the end of the first and the end of the second this was a typical hard fought derby game until the first six minutes of the third period when Durham netted four, which just left Whitley standing. The final score Durham eleven, Whitley four.

British Junior C Championship
Wembley Arena 25th April
Fife Flames...........3 Durham Mosquitoes 2 (2-0, 1-0, 0-2)
Durham Scorers: Lonsdale, Weaver 1g, Holmes 1a
Fife Scorers: M Grubb 1+1, Wood, Lynch 1g, Holmes 1a

The final takes place on Sunday 26th April with Nico Toeman again in charge with linesmen Paul Branch and Graham Horner in front of 9,000 ice hockey fans. An intensely competitive final with never more than one goal in it until 7.46 of the last period when Brebant made it 6-4 to the Wasps. Panthers came back but Ian Cooper's goal with one minute and six seconds left proved the winner for Durham 7-6. As the Ice Hockey Annual says:

"The Durham Dynasty rolls on. Wasps' victory at Wembley 92 was their fourth Heineken Championship in six attempts and gave them the league and cup double for the second straight year. It was their 14th major honour in the British League's ten seasons.

Player of the year Dan Dorion, in his first season here was twice voted Man of the Match at Wembley and was the inspiration of the Panthers. Rick Brebant who centred Wasps brilliant first line flanked by Mike Blaisdell and Ian Cooper, topped the Championship Scorers for the second successive season."

Sheffield end the season one point behind the Medway Bears, but the top four teams went into the play-offs for promotion and relegation between ED1 and Division one of the Heineken League.

English League First Division	GP	W	L	D	GF	GA	Pts
Medway Bears	32	27	3	2	369	132	56
Sheffield Steelers	32	27	4	1	378	163	55
Streatham Redskins	32	17	13	2	309	257	36
Oxford City Stars	32	17	13	2	284	221	36
Chelmsford Chieftans	32	15	14	3	277	276	33
Solihull Barons	32	13	19	0	212	271	26
Haringey Racers	32	10	22	0	193	298	20
Solent Vikings	32	8	24	0	264	453	16
Sunderland Chiefs	32	5	27	0	197	412	10

Group A finished with Medway Bears in top slot then, Trafford Metros, Streatham Redskins and bottom of the pile Oxford City Stars. Steelers in Group B were beaten in their first game at Chelmsford.

'I think Steve was ill and a couple of guys were sick but they played well in their building and they knew what they had to do and they came out winning 6-5. It wasn't a blow out. After that we were "uh-oh" we're not supposed to lose any and we were anxious for sure because we were planning on going up. We weren't planning on settling and waiting for anybody, we were going to roll over everybody we could. When it came back to it we rolled over everybody else.'

On the 4th/5th April all the seats in the Sheffield Arena are sold out again to see the final home games of the season against Chelmsford and Blackburn. On Sunday 19th of April Sheffield Steelers played their last game of the season at Blackburn Blackhawks, but so many Steelers fans travelled it was more like a home game.

So Group B of the promotion/relegation play-offs finished with the Steelers top of the pile, Chelmsford one point behind them and Blackburn Blackhawks and Livingston Kings below them with only one win each. However, controversy erupts because Phil Lee played for the Steelers when apparently he shouldn't have. It was all a mix up in paperwork, Steelers claiming never to have received notification that they shouldn't play Lee in these games. Chelmsford demand the Steelers be stripped of their points and Chelmsford promoted in their place. So the Steelers season ended as it had begun - in the hands of the BIHA. They just had to wait and see whether the decisions went in their favour.

Season 1992/93

with

Kevin Conway

Canadian forward for the Basingstoke Beavers

	GP	G	A	Pts	PIM
Heineken League	31	87	84	171	22
Benson & Hedges Cup	10	20	17	37	27
Promotion Play-Offs	6	9	6	15	2
Totals	**47**	**116**	**107**	**223**	**51**

PREMIER DIVISION: Cardiff Devils

BENSON & HEDGES CUP: Cardiff Devils

HEINEKEN CHAMPIONS: Cardiff Devils

Chapter Five

As the Cooper brothers returned to Cardiff Devils everyone expected Cardiff to do well in the Premiership this season, but few expected Division One Basingstoke to have the season they are about to have. In the summer the BIHA decide that it is Sheffield not Chelmsford who should be promoted into Division One despite playing Phil Lee when they should not have done. Sheffield are promoted with Medway Bears. Blackburn Blackhawks and Trafford Metros were the teams heading the opposite way.

As usual the Autumn Cup kicks off the season, sponsored by Benson & Hedges for the first time. This year saw all 20 teams in the Premier and Division One taking part. The top two Division One teams qualify automatically with the Premier teams whilst the remaining eight Division One teams play-off to decide the four remaining places. The teams are then divided into four roughly regionalised groups. Group A was headed by Sheffield Steelers with Ayr in second followed by Murrayfield and Fife. Whitley topped Group B with arch rivals Durham in second, Billingham and Romford below. Group C saw Norwich & Peterborough Pirates go top with Nottingham in runners-up spot. At that stage Nottingham were playing all their home games at Humberside as the ice plant at Notingham had blown up just prior to the start of the season. Humberside themselves and Medway brought up the rear in Group C. In Group D First Division Basingstoke beat Premiership Cardiff into second place with Bracknell and Slough below them.

Kevin Conway expected Basingstoke, who he played for, to do well but maybe not as well as they did.

'We knew we had a good team, but we didn't think we'd win as comfortably as we did that year. All the games were won quite easily bar just a few.'

By week nine of the season Basingstoke were the only team in the Heineken leagues with a 100% record, winning their first five games. Kevin seems to think that the players took the unbeaten run all in their stride,

'You don't really realise until everyone starts making a big issue of it, then you start thinking you've got to try a little harder to keep it going, but teams are trying a little harder to knock you off it, but it was never really an issue, though I guess it was for a lot of the fans.'

The top two teams from each group went into the quarter finals with the winner of each group taking on the runner-up from the nearest regional group, home and away. So at the beginning of October Cardiff put out the Norwich & Peterborough Pirates 14-8 on aggregate. Durham and Sheffield took it to penalty shots when 120 minutes left them tied 8-8 on aggregate, Wasps won the shoot out 3-0. Whitley put out Ayr Raiders 17-14 on aggregate, and Nottingham Panthers put out Basingstoke 10-7 away and 8-7 at home in Nottingham to take it 18-14 over-all.

Whilst the British Season gets underway, two NHL teams fly over to play in Wembley Arena as part of the NHL's European expansion plans. The Montreal Canadiens take on the Chicago Blackhawks in the Molson Challenge, a two game series on September 12th and 13th. Montreal won the first game 3-2 and the second went to Chicago on penalty shots after the game was tied 4-4. This then led to another penalty shoot-out to decide the winners of the series which went again to Chicago. The BIHA were instructed to have nothing to do with the competition by the IIHF (International Ice Hockey Federation) who were most put out that the NHL were staging a tournament in one of 'their' countries without permission. The IIHF put a ban on Wembley staging any of their international tournaments in the future.

> 'That's the BIHA for you. You can't please all the people all the time. I imagine they tried to get the IIHF to let them promote it, but I guess that never materialised. Just the way hockey goes in this country.'

October saw Durham Wasps as last year's Premier Champions taking part in the European Cup. Each round of the Cup is played in a different country in a similar fashion to the World and European Championships pools. The competition began in 1965 but the British Champions did not take part until 1983. The club sides are restricted to their league quota of imports and this together with the small squads iced in the UK has meant that no British team has progressed beyond the quarter final stage so far. This year Blackburn played host to the first round group that Durham competed in. The first quarter final group to be held in Britain ended with the British team, the Wasps, finishing third out of four, the best placing for a British team. However the first period of the last game was marred by a brawl between Wasps and Valerengen IF of Norway, with two players from each side being banished for fighting.

European Cup, Group E : Blackburn England	GP	W	L	D	GF	GA	Pts
Valeregen IF (NOR)	3	3	0	0	22	4	6
Steaua Bucharest (ROM)	3	2	1	0	17	9	4
Durham Wasps (GB)	3	1	2	0	14	14	2
Txuri Urdin (SPA)	3	0	3	0	4	30	0

On October 2nd, week seven of the British season, Bracknell beat Fife 2-0 the lowest score ever recorded in the league. On 27th Ayr Raiders are suspended from the league by the BIHA after their backer David Gardner-Brown fails to meet the deadline for paying off debts. The year had started with Ayr playing out of the new Paisley rink in front of good crowds. A new arena for Ayr called the Centrum Arena was begun in 1986 and the Ayr team changed their name from Bruins to Raiders in 1989 in the expectation that they would move to the new arena but when the owner went bust in 1990 all building work stopped. Their high hopes for 1992 finished when the statistics for Ayr's 11th season are expunged from the records and at the beginning of November Ayr are expelled from the league. Two of the Ayr imports fly home and the rest of the team find new clubs to play for, including import defenceman Chris Norton who moves to Billingham Bombers.

Basingstoke Beavers win a double header against Sheffield to go eight games into the season with eight wins. Basingstoke and Sheffield are building up a big rivalry this year as the top two teams in the First Division. Kevin believes that the building had a lot to do with Sheffield's success at that time.

'A lot of players were intimidated because of the size and they weren't used to playing in a stadium like that, particularly the British talent, and they didn't really play up to their expectations. The visitors came in and were just looking in awe, it was a good set-up how they had everything going, and the people entertained all the time. So as soon as you came in to the building they [Steelers] had a one goal lead.'

Also in November the 'Big Blue' Durham Wasps are hitting the wrong end of the Premiership table. With Rick Brebant and Tim Cranston suspended, Durham lose at home for the first time in 42 games and slip to ninth in the table. Then in the semi-finals of the Benson & Hedges Cup, Warriors knock out Durham, beating them both home (13-5) and away (3-5) in the two legged semi. In the other semi final Cardiff beat Nottingham also both home and away to take the semi 15-7. On November 23rd import forward Tim Cranston is fired from the Wasps who replace him with import defenceman Chris Norton from Billingham Bombers.

On November 22nd Tim Salmon makes his debut for the Sheffield Steelers in a 7-5 win over the Swindon Wildcats.

'The game I was supposed to play against him [Tim Salmon] I didn't play because I was injured and he didn't play either because he was injured, I think. Everyone's looking forward to that game, the game went on, obviously, but we didn't play.'

After twelve straight victories Basingstoke come undone, in the fourteenth week of the season. November 29th at Telford sees them losing game thirteen by the narrowest of margins 6-7.

December brings the final of the Benson & Hedges Cup played at the Sheffield Arena on the 12th. This was the final of 'firsts'. The first time B&H had sponsored the Cup, and also first time that the two teams, Cardiff and Whitley had made it to the final of the Autumn Cup competition. The two teams at that time were one and two in the league. A crowd of 4800 saw the first period tied at two all. Cardiff took the second 1-2, and then in the third they pulled away 1-6. The man of the match awards went to two young players whose names will appear more and more frequently as we progress through the seasons. For the Whitley Warriors, local hero David Longstaff and for the Cardiff Devils, again a local lad, Nicky Chinn.

After seven years with the Nottingham Panthers, in December GB coach Alex Dampier moves on to become coach of Sheffield Steelers in Division One. Nottingham sign Kevin Murphy to replace Dampier. In Billingham Terry Matthews is tempted out of retirement to coach, whilst Durham release forward Mick Blaisdell and sign Ukrainian Sergi Gavrilenko.

The new Paisley ice rink was opened in August and played host to the Ayr Raiders for the beginning of the season. December 20th saw a Scottish select side take on a new team, Paisley Pirates, the Pirates won 8-2. Despite their late start Paisley were able to join the Scottish League (equivalent to English League Division ELD1), and ran away with the league title!

At the beginning of the New Year Cardiff were top of the Premier Division despite having played the fewest games.

Heineken British League Premier Division	GP	W	L	D	GF	GA	Pts
Cardiff Devils	17	13	3	1	146	84	27
Murrayfield Racers	19	12	6	1	174	133	25
Whitley Warriors	20	11	9	0	146	160	22
Bracknell Bees	20	9	9	2	114	109	20
Fife Flyers	22	10	12	0	131	144	20
Humberside Seahawks	18	9	9	0	105	104	18
Durham Wasps	18	8	9	1	121	111	17
Nottingham Panthers	19	7	10	2	138	153	16
Norwich & P'boro Pirates	18	7	11	0	114	134	14
Billingham Bombers	21	5	13	3	148	205	13

A new year was no help to the ailing Durham Wasps and on January 10th Billingham Bombers beat the Wasps for the first time in the Heineken League. That was the first time in *forty-five* games between the two teams. After an off-ice dispute with Trafford over the signing of Ukrainian Oleg Sinkov, which Durham lost, Durham were given special dispensation to sign Dan Fascinato, who became the last import to be signed this season. But Durham slump to a record 12th straight defeat the next week. Kevin Conway who had played a season for the Wasps in the glory years has mixed feelings about Durham

> 'It was an excellent team to play for because they always won, but none of his [Tom Smith] players got paid very well and he kept on changing his imports quite often. Even though they were winning every year he would change one or two imports. Tom didn't like anyone who speaks their mind, you just had to be quiet and do what you were told.'

The Guildford Spectrum multi-sport complex opened in February, but the rink opened earlier to allow the new Ice Hockey team, the Guilford Flames, to start competing in the English League. Their first game was 23rd January and the first goal was scored by the Flames after only 1.33 minutes against the Stevenage Sharks. The Spectrum rink has a capacity of 2,200 and 2,139 saw this first game, go to the Flames 13-3.

On January 30th Scotland beat England in the 50th Home International which was hosted by the Sheffield Arena. But how does Kevin Conway qualify as an honorary Scot?

> 'I think it was because I played a year in Ayr and I guess I was the candidate of the moment. At the time they were probably a good idea, as time goes on things

change. It was rivalry to build up each year, like the rugby, and a few other sports, the fans love the England v Scotland games. It was good fun I think.'

The next night saw Basingstoke away in Sheffield.

'Obviously Basingstoke and Sheffield were one and two and I think we built up a big rivalry there because of the two teams getting promoted and stuff.'

The Beavers beat Sheffield in this one to take a massive twelve point lead in Division One.

Young British Player of the Year: Damian Smith of Durham Wasps

Kevin Conway on Damian Smith
'Damian Smith, a good smooth skater, good with the puck. When I played in Durham he didn't get on much, but a few years after that he was a really good player, a lot of points and goals. He probably still would be if he was still playing the game. He was a lot different player than Paul, his elder brother, he was a little bit more physical. The players liked Damian because of his personality, and the way he carried himself, Damian was probably one of the best Smiths to get along with.'

The main news in February came on the 16th when Heineken announced that their 10 year, £5 million sponsorship of the national league will cease this season at the end of the Wembley Championship Play-offs.

'Heineken put a lot of money into the sport but I hear that they weren't too keen on the way the league was run and they pulled out because of it. Maybe a lot of other sponsors got turned away because they asked Heineken what was it like to sponsor ice hockey and Heineken probably didn't put in a good word for us. Its a shame things didn't work out.'

There had been many awards for the players and coaches sponsored by Heineken, like the monthly coaching, points scorer and shutouts awards.

'As David [Graham] told you, players will try a little harder, goalies had something to try for. Not many goalies were making good sums of money back then, and it was good to finish first in the scoring for £250 or something like that. Little incentives like that get the best out of players.'

Also in February, on the 14th Basingstoke clinch Division One with five weeks to spare. On 21st Durham Wasps were shut-out at home by the Cardiff Devils 7-0, Jason Wood was between the pipes for Cardiff. Six days later on 27th Cardiff clinch their second Heineken Premier League title.

March began badly for the British Ice Hockey community when on 7th leading British Referee Mick Curry was killed in a car crash, on his way home from officiating the game between Norwich & Peterborough Pirates and Humberside Seahawks. Linesman Sean Byrne was also injured in the crash.

'I remember Mick quite well and then you hear that he's been in a car crash and he's been killed. You just don't believe it until you don't see him no more and then it starts hitting you. We weren't close but I knew him from talking to him on the ice, its just an emptiness that can't be replaced. You don't like that happening to anyone involved in the game. It was a sad day.'

The late Mick Curry, referee killed in a car accident

the Wasps, was the only player to play every game in the teams ten years of Heineken league sponsorship, and he, it would appear, felt the need to protest at the infamy of his last game.

> *'Bennett was just sitting in the middle of the ice after the game was called and wouldn't leave the ice. Ivor was a bit of a comedian but he'd give you 110% every game, he didn't like what was happening so he had to express his disapproval of the ref-ing and the way the game got called.'*

So top of Group A to take the promotion spot are the Basingstoke Beavers with the Wasps in second place. Group B of the promotion play-offs saw fellow Division One team Sheffield Steelers top the table after signing Canadian Todd Bidner of Humberside to cover for injured Scott Neil. Sheffield were allowed to replace the Scottish born and bred Neil with an import as Neil was in the top twenty scorers and Bidner was considered a fair replacement by the authorities. Bidner was to become a Steelers favourite after those few short weeks with the team as the play-off competition went right down to the last game at Milton Keynes Kings which Sheffield won 5-3. (in goal for MKK, David Graham) Sheffield had achieved the unique double of promotion in successive years.

But as the promotion play-offs began there were rumours that the Premier Division was to expand next season, and this, so the rumour went, had something to do with the Durham Wasps being bottom of the pile.

> *'Everyone wanted to see Durham go down, to see if it ever did materialise because we knew Tom had a lot of pull in British Ice Hockey back then. They were almost like a superpower of British Ice Hockey, teams like Durham and Murrayfield. Even the fans were saying, except the Durham fans, that they would have liked to see them go down. But Tom would buy a team and they would clobber everyone and they'd be right back up, so you don't know if it was for the better.'*

At the other end of the Premier table the top eight teams were in the Championship Play-offs with the winners of the league, Cardiff Devils, tipped to make it the Grand Slam. The Play-offs had to be squeezed into twelve days due to GB competing in Pool B and as Sheffield lost Scott Neil to injury so Nottingham Panthers replaced GB defender Chris Kelland. Controversially they replaced him with 'Super Forward', Steve Moria. A move Ok'd by the BIHA but considered an unfair exchange by some. The eight teams started in two groups. Table toppers in Group A were the conquering Cardiff Devils whilst in second place were lowly Humberside Seahawks who had only just made it into the competition. Group B went to Nottingham Panthers with Murrayfield in second spot.

The first semi-final is played on Friday 23rd April at Wembley Arena, with the teams that finished one and two in the league expected to make a real game of it. But it turned into a thrashing when the Devils went three up in the first period whilst Murrayfield's only contribution was to take three penalties. In the end Cardiff ran out 9-0 winners. Jason Wood was between the pipes for Cardiff as they produced the first Wembley finals shut-out, against the competition's highest scorer, Tony Hand, who topped the scorers without taking a single point in the final weekend.

The second semi-final took place on Saturday 24th April between Humberside and Nottingham. This game was much tighter, with the Humberside team lifted by the underdogs title. The first period ended one each, with eight penalties called. The second period was taken by Humberside 3-1 and the third by Nottingham 2-0 to take it into ten minutes sudden death over time. Despite six attempts on the Humberside goal it was Humberside who put one past Ian Young in the Nottingham net at 6.36 to make it to the final.

British Junior C Championship
Wembley Arena 24th April

Fife Flames...........2   Durham Mosquitoes 5 (1-0, 3-1, 1-0)
Durham Scorers: Lonsdale, Weaver 2a, Holmes 2+1, Carter 1+1, Knights 1g, B Watkins & T Watkins 1a
Fife Scorers: Reid 1g, Maxwell 1g, Dunbar 1a

The final was on Sunday 25th April. Referee in charge is Glen Meier with linesmen Simon Kirkham and Paul Branch. A capacity crowd of 9,018 saw Cardiff take the first period 1-0 and then go four up in the first six minutes of the second period. Perhaps the two teams performances were a reflection of their semi-final experiences, the Humberside Seahawks suffering after their epic battle with Nottingham the night before. The 'Hawks cause suffered further when Paul Simpson had his shoulder broken in the first period, leaving the 'Hawks with only three defencemen. The final score 7-4 to Cardiff. This shows the power of the Cooper brothers. It was their 6th Championship in seven years, their second with the Devils, the rest with the Wasps.

Coach of the year for the Premier went to John Lawless of the all-conquering Cardiff Devils, whilst for Division One it went to Peter Woods of the all-conquering Basingstoke Beavers.

> *'Two respected coaches back then who deserved the credibility that they got. Especially with the two teams winning their divisions so comfortably there were probably no other coaches even close to getting the awards.*
>
> *Back then Peter was probably the best coach in the country with his credentials. He was the first coach to introduce practice, instead of scrimmages at practice, which is what most coaches used to do because they were player coaches. Playing under him you never had a scrimmage, it was good to get back to practice. He showed a lot of the British players what to do and how to do it; a lot of the flow drills instead of stopping and waiting for the puck or working up and down the wings. He created a lot for the British players to utilise the whole of the big ice surfaces we were playing on.'*

During the summer it becomes apparent that the BIHA had been talking to Peter Woods with a view to him becoming director of coaching for them, but the BIHA could not come up with a firm offer quick enough when Woods is offered a job in Norway, so he takes the Norwegian offer and leaves the country.

Season 1993/94
with
Todd Bidner
Canadian forward for the
Teesside Bombers

	GP	G	A	Pts	PIM
Promotion Play-Off	6	10	7	17	6
Premier League	36	49	31	80	108
Benson & Hedges Cup	Injured and without a team				
Totals	42	59	38	97	114

PREMIER DIVISION: Cardiff Devils

BENSON & HEDGES CUP: Murrayfield Racers

HEINEKEN CHAMPIONS: Cardiff Devils

Chapter Six

The 1993 season started early, not with the Autumn Cup but with the GB team in the first round of the Olympic Qualifying tournament. There were four additional dual nationals added to the team that iced for GB and won promotion to Pool A last season. One of those four was Todd Bidner. Todd first came to Britain to play for Fife in the 1985/86 season and went on to play for Peterborough for the next four years before stints at Telford, Nottingham, Bracknell and Humberside. He was one of a tiny handful of players coming to this country at that time with NHL experience, having played one season for the Washington Capitals. Playing for GB obviously reminded him of his early career in the pro-leagues stateside.

> *'I loved to play in that tournament because it was the first time in a long time I had played at that intensive calibre of hockey. Even though the competition was out of our league it was still fun to be a part of a full 20 player squad … practising every day, eating together as a team and of course having a beer with the boys at the end of the day. I guess I was proud to play for Great Britain since I believe if it wasn't for the pro's like myself, Ronny Plumb and Gary Unger, all of which had played in the NHL, British Ice Hockey might have taken longer to develop to the stage it is at now.'*

The qualifying tournament was made up of the winners and runners up from European Pool B, Great Britain and Poland, Pool C winners Latvia, and Asian Cup winners, Japan. Then the IIHF granted a place to Slovakia due to the political changes in the former Czechoslovakia. The tournament was hosted by Britain at the Sheffield Arena and organised by Orbit International who also organised the Heineken Championships.

The only warm-up game before the tournament was against Dutch First Division side Geleen and the GB team blot their copybook when only sixteen players turn up. All the Cardiff players are with their team playing a 'Charity Shield' game against Durham and GB Coach Alex Dampier is also otherwise engaged as he takes Sheffield Steelers to play a friendly against Trafford.

The first game of the tournament was a draw with Poland, the Polish net minder keeping them in the game in the second period. Final shots on goal; 23 on GB McCrone and 39 on Jaworski in the Polish net. Next up were the Japanese who proved to be fast and agile skaters also capable of playing the physical game that GB brought to them. Japan went on to win 4-2. This was the first defeat of the British Squad in a full international in two and a half years.

The next game was against the Latvians who were tipped to be at the top of the pile. The GB squad went 2-0 up, Todd Bidner scoring the first after 40 seconds, then the Latvians brought it back to 4-4 until the 39th minute. Then the lack of preparation showed as the GB team went down 8-4 and the Olympic dream was over. "We ran out of gas" said Coach Alex Dampier after the game.

The last game for GB was Slovakia, a side with many ex-NHL players and some currently still in that top flight. The home team went down playing hard, and defending doggedly.

Britain's only goal of the game came from a break down the wing from man of the match (for the second time) Doug McEwen, who then netted his own rebound.

Tim Cranston made the most of having the top British players in one place at the Olympic tournament, getting the Players Association up and running again, with their first meeting in many years. Tim said "We have taken the sport to the brink of the Olympics, now I and many other players feel it is time for us to make our voices heard."

The Players Association was a double edged sword for Todd.

> *Tim did a great job getting the guys that had put a lot of years and time into developing the league not only at the Premier level, but the junior level as well. We put in a lot of extra time with the kids. The Players Association was put together to help players establish themselves as Canadian/British on an international level. I think it helped make the league respectable in the eyes of Europe, but it opened the doors for people with British passports to come into the UK and play as a Brit without really paying any dues to the league or country. That kind of burns some of us to see our jobs go when we put a lot of time and effort into the quality of the game in Britain.'*

On May 10th the BIHA had announced that the Premier Division is to expand by two teams, so despite failing in the promotion/relegation play-offs Durham are still a Premier team. There were to be sixteen teams in Division One divided into two regionalised groups. Although the BIHA said this expansion was due to a need to restructure the leagues, few seemed to argue that the main reason was to keep relegated Durham Wasps in the top flight.

> *'It just goes to show that the BIHA and Tom Smith were one and the same. Rules change to suit who the BIHA want it to suit.'*

It had been decided in the summer that the import rules would change so that each team was allowed five imports. Only three imports are allowed to ice per game, (no change) but there could be up to five foreign trained players when other categories are taken into account. The changes were partly due to pressure from the Players Association.

Another rule introduced this year was a wage cap of £150,000 for each club. On breaking the rules a club would be fined £5,000 and have five points deducted, a second offence would produce another fine (amount not specified) and a loss of eight points.

The season gets under way for the Premier teams at the same time as the NHL bring the New York Rangers and the Toronto Maple Leafs to Wembley on 11th and 12th of September. The BIHA refuse to co-operate as directed by its governing body the IIHF, so there was no attempt, once again, to use the best league in the world to promote the British game.

'This just shows you the ignorance of the BIHA not to acknowledge the best hockey in the world and as a result I don't know if the NHL has been back since. Maybe they [BIHA] didn't want people to see how good hockey can be played and how bad British Ice Hockey was at the time! They should have made it a huge extravaganza, if anything, just to educate the people more.'

The first round of the Autumn Cup, sponsored by Benson & Hedges, is divided into four groups with all twelve Premier Division teams and the top teams from Division One. Group A was topped by Murrayfield Racers with old rivals Durham Wasps in second slot. Group B was taken by the Humberside Hawks, whilst Teesside Bombers found themselves bottom, having lost all six games. Nottingham Panthers won Group C with Slough Jets in second spot. In Group D Cardiff Devils beat Basingstoke Beavers in to second place.

Dan Fowler, Todd Humphrey and Chad Thompson never saw out the B&H games at Teesside.

'The team was promised money that they never got from the council so the team couldn't afford players that weren't really that effective on the ice anyway so they had to go.'

A sign of what was to happen to Teesside throughout this season. First new recruit was Scott Young who had been planning a year in Dutch hockey, but the team went bankrupt two weeks before he was due to come over. With a ticket that had already been paid for Scott decided to come to Europe and look for a job. His friend Mike Bishop, playing in Humberside, put him in touch with Terry Matthews, Teesside coach, and now he is a Bomber.

With the name Bombers, based at Billingham Forum, you'd expect it to be the Billingham Bombers. Well it was originally and then it became the Cleveland Bombers, but with the prospect of Cleveland ceasing to exist, the name was changed again, to Teesside!

On October 4th the Peterborough ice rink suddenly closes for 'refurbishment', but it becomes clear very quickly that there is no intention of re-opening it, the owners claim that the rink is losing too much money. Milton Keynes rink had also closed at short notice in the summer. Tony Oliver in Milton Keynes and David Thorpe in Peterborough both masterminded returns, the Bladerunner rink in Milton Keynes opening in time for the beginning of this season. Obviously, David Thorpe had a slightly more tricky job, keeping the team going whilst working on re-opening the rink. This task was not helped by the fact that 17 miles of refrigeration piping had already been ripped up. Once work began, Pirates fans and players also had to guard the rink at night after the place was vandalised. Some of the imports found themselves with unexpected day jobs working on the site! The Peterborough Pirates were without ice for 77 days and played all their games away, training when and where they could with late night trips to Chelmsford, Nottingham and Milton Keynes. The ice pad is reduced in size by nine feet all round, replacing the boards and installing 500 new seats. The work also saw the end of the famous mid ice slope that was Peterborough's claim to fame prior to the closure.

From the 8th to 10th of October Cardiff Devils were in Latvia in the quarter finals of the European Cup. Cardiff won one game against the Lithuanian Champions, and finished third from four with all the other teams ex-Soviet block (Latvia, Lithuania and Ukraine). Hilton Ruggles picked up the award for tournament top scorer. Four players had scored seven points but Hilton was the only one with five goals. As Hilton himself pointed out, with other European teams playing four line hockey, he had more ice time than most to clock up his goals.

Back in Teesside things are still not going well for the Bombers. They face newly promoted Basingstoke at home on October 10th, Basingstoke's first league game in the top flight and Basingstoke win 11-8. This game is the first appearance of new import, Igor Slivinsky, a Ukrainian winger for Teesside. The end of the month sees the arrival of Todd Bidner and Jim Pennycook to bolster the ranks. Up until this point in the season Todd has not been able to find a team in Britain to play for despite his experience and talent.

'I broke my ribs against Holland playing for GB and it was just pretty tough to find a team. Not that I was asking for a bunch of money or anything! Then Billingham called because Jeff Lindsay got hurt.'

Todd Bidner with Teesside

For Teesside there are problems with the work permit for Slivinsky, and he is forced to sit out several games.

The end of October sees the quarter finals of the B&H Cup. Cardiff Devils beat Slough Jets at home to go through after drawing the first game away at Slough. Durham Wasps put out Humberside Seahawks. Murrayfield Racers just go through against Whitley Warriors with only one goal separating the teams after two games 16-15. Similarly Nottingham go through by one goal over Basingstoke Beavers 6-5.

The semi finals of the cup are played on the 6th and 13th November. Murrayfield Racers versus the Durham Wasps is live on Sky television and Durham re-capture their old BBC TV jinx and go down 11-3. They can then only manage a 6-6 draw at home and Murrayfield go through to the finals in December. In the other semi, Nottingham win the first game at home 5-4 but Cardiff win at home by a greater margin and go through 11-9 overall.

On November 20th the Bombers lost 12-6 to the Murrayfield Racers, but three of the Teesside players give the fans something to celebrate. Todd Bidner scores his 450th British League goal, Jim Pennycook scored his 250th league point and Paul Davison notched up his 200th point.

The final of the B&H cup is played on 4th December at the Sheffield Arena. Murrayfield Racers take a three to nil lead into the first break despite Cardiff out shooting them 16-12. Moray Hanson between the pipes for Murrayfield kept out the Cardiff attack until the 57th minute when Nicky Chinn put one past him. Then Rick Brebant made it two for Cardiff, but Lindsay Lovell, Tony Hand and Chris Palmer had already doubled Murrayfields tally, giving a final score of 6-2 to Murrayfield.

On December 12th Teesside Bombers play local rivals Whitley Warriors. Warriors go 4-0 up in the first period and then midway through the second Stephen Johnson is sent to the dressing room with a misconduct penalty, then Scott Young follows. Jeff Lindsay then decides to show his sense of humour by waving a towel on a stick as the white flag of surrender to the Whitley Warriors. Unfortunately for the team, referee Graham Horner doesn't see it that way and sends Lindsay to the early shower as well. However the young Teesside players stepped up and the only goal after that is a penalty shot from Whitley Warrior Scott Morrison, giving Whitley a 5-2 final score. This game saw the unveiling of Whitley Warriors new digital clock, replacing the old sweep-hand clock that had been in service for 38 years. These old sweep-hand clocks, also seen at Durham and Fife, were always one of the away team's pet hates as it was nearly impossible to follow.

Heavy snow that night had led to the Sheffield versus Basingstoke and Humberside versus Fife games to be called off. Unfortunately the message didn't reach Basingstoke - already on the road - and they made it all the way through the snow to the Sheffield Arena!

Peterborough Pirates return to their newly refurbished rink mid-way through December and lose 9-5 against Durham. At the time Pirates Captain, Mark Mackie, told Powerplay

1993/94

Magazine " In a funny sort of way the result doesn't really matter, we're back and that's all we're thinking about at the moment."

On 27th December Humberside Hawks play host to the struggling Bombers. Unfortunately for the Bombers, Hawks mark up their biggest ever score in the Premier League with a 16-0 win. Two nights later, five hundred and twenty-five fans at Billingham Forum, home to the Teesside Bombers, see the home side beat Nottingham Panthers 8-7. The win owes much to the netminding of Peter Graham, and the early hat trick from Todd Bidner.

'Hockey is a funny game and when people say that anyone can win on any given night , that's exactly what happened. I really don't think Nottingham was up for this game and expected to walk all over us.'

The Bombers problems return as netminder Peter Graham leaves the club.

'It was a big blow to the team but again it was all down to money - if a player gets his wages cut he's probably going to look for another team which is what I think happened in Peter's case.'

This puts increasing pressure on Teesside's remaining experienced goalie Ian Young.

'I think Ian Young did just fine when Peter left.'

The league table going into Christmas saw Fife Flyers at the top of the Premier and Teesside at the bottom. Top of the scoring chart is Murrayfield's Tony Hand and top of the netminding averages is John 'Bernie' McCrone of Fife. Fife kick off the New Year with a 7-6 win over local rivals Murrayfield on 4th January but the game is disrupted by the crowd. Both teams are sent to the dressing rooms after Paul Pentland is struck by a coin thrown from the crowd. The crowd were warned that any repeat would lead to the game being finished in an empty building. At 57.45 it was the teams that disrupted the game with one player ejected from the game for fighting, and three other penalties on Fife, giving Racers a five on three powerplay. Fife defended until 35 seconds remained when Richard Laplante scored. But it was too little too late and Fife held on to the game.

British League Premier Division	GP	W	L	D	GF	GA	Pts
Fife Flyers	19	14	4	1	137	69	29
Cardiff Devils	16	12	4	0	119	77	24
Murrayfield Racers	17	11	4	2	147	100	24
Durham Wasps	16	11	4	1	133	80	23
Whitley Warriors	17	8	6	3	102	92	19
Sheffield Steelers	17	8	6	3	113	87	19
Nottingham Panthers	16	9	6	1	88	78	19
Basingstoke Beavers	17	5	9	3	98	119	13
Humberside Hawks	16	5	10	1	87	102	11
Bracknell Bees	18	5	12	1	81	130	11
Peterborough Pirates	18	3	13	2	80	166	8
Teesside Bombers	19	3	16	0	99	184	6

January also sees a small ray of hope as the council grant Teesside Bombers £20,000.

'I don't think the team got all of that money at once, so it really didn't help the team too much. Guys like Dave Rennison and Morris Moore put a lot of their own money in to keep everybody paid and to keep the team operating.'

On January 20th the BIHA announce the appointment of David Frame as the first Chief Executive of the Association, his appointment is to commence on March 1st. Frame is a Scotsman who moved to the BIHA from the Brent Walker Organisation in Cardiff, where he was Director of Marketing. He had experience of ice hockey through his work with Cardiff Devils who were owned by Brent Walker.

'David Frame was probably the only man available at the time, since Mike O'Connor turned the job down. I think if Mike had taken the job the league may be set up different today.'

Murrayfield played host to the 51st Home International on January 29th and the game was also televised on BBC 'Grandstand'. However six of the England team fail to show including, Stephen Cooper, David Longstaff, and Damian Smith, and both sides use import players. The BIHA were again criticised for not gaining a sponsor for a game with terrestrial TV coverage.

The next night two new imports made their debuts for the Teesside Bombers, Tim Delay and Dan Pompeo. This game against the Humberside Hawks saw the Bombers beaten with the highest aggregate score of the season in the Premiership 19-9. February begins with strange things going on in Murrayfield as the team 'do a runner' from the Murrayfield Rink and take all their kit to Livingston. Five days later with help from the BIHA they move back to Murrayfield. In Teesside Terry Matthews announces he is giving up the job of Bombers coach to concentrate on his own business commitments. Todd Bidner and Scott Young agree to take on the extra responsibility of coaching, whilst still playing, for the rest of the season.

'Well it was down to money again. The management had to stop paying Terry so he had to put more time into his business to make up the difference.'

The end of February sees Kevin Conway of Basingstoke and Paul Adey of Nottingham put out with potentially season ending injuries. Bad news for their teams and for GB. Kevin suffered a broken leg after 22 seconds of Basingstoke's match against Humberside. Paul Adey's injury was to his knee after an alleged 'submarine' hit from Whitley Warriors Terry Ord. In this check, instead of hitting body to body, a player drops down to knee height to make contact and stop his opposing player. Nottingham Panther's coach Mike Blaisdell was outraged by the nature of the check, claiming that no professional should use such a check since the most likely outcome is a serious injury and players should respect each others need to make a living. Warriors coach Peter Bender said that Nottingham had just taken exception to a hard hitting game. The game ended with referee, John Moore, handing out 162 minutes in penalties.

The beginning of March sees Teesside end a fifteen game losing streak when they beat fellow strugglers Peterborough 10-6. Seven days later Dan Pompeo and Tim Delay walk out, leaving Scott Young and Todd Bidner as the only imports for the Billingham team.

'They weren't very good. This wasn't their type of league. Still, Scott Young and myself had to take a pay cut so the team could finish out the season.'

And see out the season they did, but what got them motivated to go out and play after fifteen defeats?

'Not much, it was so frustrating. To know you just had seven or eight guys on the team and to know that you had to play 50 minutes of the game, well Scott played more because he never came off the ice. We just tried to make it as respectable as we could. Oh we had fun with it and I think all the teams that came in to play us knew us as players and respected us as players and for sticking the season out. They didn't want to kill us that's for sure.

There was Scott, myself and Jim Pennycock, and we lived over a Pub. That's why we stayed, because we lived over the top of Flannigans Pub in Stockton and they had strippers every Wednesday night!!'

On March 18th Nottingham joined the list of financially struggling teams, announcing that if they failed to raise £20,000 in a fortnight they would be forced to pull out of the play-offs. The fans and the stadium rally round and sort the problems out over the weekend.

Young British Player of the Year :
David Longstaff of Whitley Warriors

Todd Bidner on David Longstaff
'David is a strong hockey player. Its too bad he didn't get the coaching he needed before going to training camp. You never know, with his size and strength, he might have stayed there.'

This was the last year for the Young British Player of the Year award after nine years. None of the British youngsters had taken up offers to stay and both the Calgary Flames and the government of Alberta thought the time had come to end the programme.

Two days before the final weekend of the season, the BIHA decide that both the Sheffield Steelers and the Murrayfield Racers have broken the wage capping regulations and the BIHA will penalise the teams by docking five points. Steelers immediately apply for an injunction against the decision, apparently due to its possible effect on their play-off group, although as it turns out it would have little effect.

So, on to the last league games of the season. Tony Hand retains his Premier Division scoring title and Patrick Scott takes the Division One title with a record 262 points.

'Tony Hand is a great player, he has always played hard. Its too bad he didn't give himself a legitimate shot at playing pro in North America. If anyone could have played in the NHL he could have.'

Meanwhile, with a hat trick in the last game of the regular season, Todd Bidner scored his 1000th point in the British League, joining an elite band of only nine players who have reached the huge 1000th point mark. This brings his tally for league games (excluding cups and play-offs) to, 285 games in nine seasons with 492 goals 510 assists for 1002 points at the end of the season.

'I guess that was a lot of points considering the amount of games I had played. But you have to remember that in some of those games, scores were 15-0 which meant a lot of points that were insignificant goals and assists and I never was much for goal scoring titles.'

Players' Player of the Year and Best British Defenceman both go to Stephen Cooper of the Cardiff Devils. The British Ice Hockey Writers Association's Player of the Year goes to Doug Smail of Fife. Coach of the Year goes to John Lawless also of the Cardiff Devils. The Mick Curry Memorial Trophy for most improved official goes to Simon Kirkham.

British League Premier Division	GP	W	L	D	GF	GA	Pts
Cardiff Devils	44	39	5	0	422	220	78
Fife Flyers	44	27	15	2	304	192	56
Sheffield Steelers *	44	28	12	4	313	198	55
Nottingham Panthers	44	26	16	2	288	224	54
Murrayfield Racers *	44	27	15	2	385	286	51
Durham Wasps	44	24	18	2	385	286	50
Whitley Warriors	44	22	18	4	282	298	48
Humberside Hawks	44	18	22	4	301	308	40
Basingstoke Beavers	44	12	25	6	255	344	30
Bracknell Bees	44	11	30	3	220	320	25
Peterborough Pirates	44	9	32	3	239	398	21
Teesside Bombers	44	5	39	0	238	491	10

teams with 5 points deducted for wage capping violation

The play-off groups of the Championship final start with Cardiff Devils in Group A alongside Nottingham Panthers, Whitley Warriors and Durham Wasps. Group B has the Sheffield Steelers, the Fife Flyers, Murrayfield Racers and Humberside Hawks. Racers play their first home play-off game at the Murrayfield rink but then the rink announce that they have withdrawn all facilities from the team. Racers play both their away and home games against Fife in the Fife rink at Kirkcaldy and lose twice, although they then play Humberside at Livingston and win 15-5. The two losses to Fife put paid to their chances and Fife go through with Sheffield to the Wembley weekend. In Group A Cardiff sweep through the opposition winning five and drawing with Wasps at Durham.

1993/94

Wasps, Warriors and Panthers were all in with a chance but, despite still being without star import Paul Adey, the Nottingham Panthers get the points and go through.

Division One had been expanded in 93/94 from nine to sixteen teams and divided into regional groups. Each team played those in its region twice home and away and those in the other division once home and away. The team with the most points was deemed to be the Division One Champions, and this honour went to Milton Keynes Kings in Division One North. Slough Jets were top of Division One South. For the promotion/relegation play-offs Teesside Bombers from the Premier were put in Group A with the overall champions and two others and Peterborough Pirates went into Group B with Slough Jets.

Winners in Group A, Milton Keynes Kings gain promotion. MKK only lost one game in the series. Unfortunately Teesside Bombers only managed one win out of six, against the Telford Tigers with Scott Young netting five goals and Todd Bidner netting four to win that game 12-9.

> *'A result of the diminishing team we had. I think we only played with two imports and six others.'*

This left Teesside bottom of the table and playing Division One hockey next season, not entirely surprising after all the trauma and upheaval throughout the year, but Todd and Scott Young are still there battling for the team to the end.

> *'We just stuck it out to finish out the season. You hear that Stockton Council are going to give some money, but they never ever did and it was past deadline day so we couldn't go anywhere else. We had a lot of fun in Stockton and then I went back to University, at Teesside Uni, so I was up there anyway going to school. We had a good time, I liked the North-East.'*

Todd Binder watching from the other side of the plexi

Table toppers in Group B were the Peterborough Pirates although Slough pushed them all the way.

The first Wembley without Heineken Sponsorship began on Saturday 23rd April with the Cardiff Devils taking on the Fife Flyers. The first goal went to Cardiff after just ten seconds as Hilton Ruggles hit the first of his three goals. The Devils took the first period 6-3 giving Fife a mountain to climb, the second ended even 1-1 then the Devils took the third to win 9-5.

The second semi-final saw local rivals Nottingham Panthers take on Sheffield Steelers who had made it to Wembley in only their third year. Neil Abel, Les Millie and Tim Cranston put the Steelers three nil up in the first period. Three more for Steelers in the second period, and Millie started the third period by scoring his hat trick goal. A final goal from Tommy Plommer left the shattered Panthers on the wrong side of an 8-0 score line.

British Junior C Championship
Wembley Arena 24th April

Fife Flames...........1   Swindon Leopards ....1 (0-1, 0-0, 0-1 OT 0-0)
Swindon Scorers: Lee Braithwaite 1g, Neil Liddiard 1a
Fife Scorers: Lee Mercer 1g, John Robertson 1a

The Junior final, held on the morning of the Championship final, ended in a 1-1 draw after five minutes of overtime so the trophy was shared between Swindon, who were playing their first Junior Final, and Fife Flames who were playing in their fifth consecutive final. It turned out to be the most evenly balanced game of the weekend.

Cardiff Devils dismissed the Steelers in the final as the Steelers had done the Nottingham Panthers in the semi-final the day before. Referee for the final was Ken Taggart with Andy Carson and Gordon Pirry the linesmen as 8,968 fans watched the Devils take the game easily. Import defenceman Selmar Odelein of the Steelers had been suffering for some time with a bad back. He and the team knew he would play only one game over the weekend, he played in the Nottingham game. The next morning he had to be helped out of his bed by his team mates, the morning of the final, and although he skated in the warm-up he was unable to play a part in the game. Whether this one player would have made a significant difference to the final outcome is hard to say, but maybe it was a reflection of Steelers' expectations. They came to play the semi-final in their first year at Wembley, but when they reached the final they seemed surprised to be there and eventually shocked by the result.

Cardiff Devils beat the Sheffield Steelers 12 -1, the largest winning margin in the eleven years of the Championships at Wembley and the first time any team had reached double figures. Man of the Match for Cardiff, Nicky Chinn, became the first player to score four goals in a final. The massive Steelers support managed to keep singing. Despite what everyone had predicted three years ago when the Steelers were formed, the Steelers fans were getting used to coming second, second to Medway Bears in

ELD1, second to Basingstoke in Division One and now second in their first Wembley Championships. The other fans saw it differently and took great delight in singing 'What a waste of money'.

Wembley is a unique sporting occasion. When the tickets go on sale any four out of eight teams might make the final and so there is a large cross section of fans from all eight of these teams as well as fans of hockey from the other teams and leagues, and the banter remains, on the whole light hearted. Not only are there fans from all of ice hockey, during the Heineken years there was also plenty to attract the players who were not playing to attend, so fans and players rubbed shoulders, shared beers and rumours. As Todd said

> *'I've been to Wembley a number of times to watch, but it was usually from the Heineken area so I can't comment on the games, but it sure was always a great party!'*

The end of the season was still a little way off for those in the GB squad. They flew out to Bolzano in Italy to take on the best Ice Hockey Nations in the World Championship Pool A. The selected team includes fifteen dual nationals and eight British born and trained players. This time the GB team did not include Todd Bidner and this was mainly his choice.

> *'I think I was bitter at the time with the BIHA because I had played at the beginning of the year in the Olympic qualifying tournament and after the tournament I could not seem to find a place to play anywhere because of the changing of the import rules, which seem to change every year anyway to suit them.'*

For Pool A of the tournament the teams are divided into two groups for the Qualifying Round, then the top two teams in each Group play-off in semifinal and final, whilst the bottom two play-off to see who gets relegated. GB were in Group A.

The first game of the tournament for GB was on the 26th April against the reigning World Champions, Russia, and almost half the squad had been playing at Wembley some 48 hours before. Russia win 12-3. Ice Hockey News Review reported "Stephen Cooper summed up the British mood when he pointed out that he was neither angry nor disappointed when Valeri Kamensky skated smoothly past him on one occasion. 'I just wanted to drop my gloves and give him a round of applause. He was so good.'"

As the debate over using dual nationals in the GB team rumbles ever on, it is interesting to note that at this Pool A there are 51 Canadian born players playing for teams other than Canada, and one British born player, Steve Thomas (born in Stockport), playing for the Canadians.

GBs' next game is against Germany the following day and again they are beaten, this time 4-0. On the 29th they take on Italy and are beaten 10-2. Then on April 30th GB played the mighty Canadians and the dual national contingent are certainly 'up' for this game. Rick Brebant (born in Canada) picked up Man of the Match for GB whilst Steve Thomas (born in Britain) picked up Man of the Match for Canada! The team representing Canada win 8-2.

The next game was against Austria, a team where GB hoped to gain some points, however the Austrians were much improved and GB went down 10-0 and into the relegation play-off with Norway. This appeared to be the only game where an inquest was justified, the Norwegians were bigger and faster than GB, but only just and GB were more skilful. The Norwegians won 5-2 assisted by too many minutes penalty killing by the GB team. Great Britain return straight back to Pool B as Switzerland who were relegated last year return straight back to Pool A.

World & European Championship: Pool A	Group A						
	GP	W	L	D	GF	GA	Pts
Canada	5	5	0	0	24	7	10
Russia	5	4	1	0	30	7	8
Italy	5	3	2	0	17	15	6
Austria	5	1	3	1	15	15	3
Germany	5	1	3	1	9	14	3
Great Britain	5	0	5	0	7	44	0

As the hockey season came to an end there were still one or two matters for the BIHA to sort out, like what was going on at Murrayfield? The BIHA also won their court battle with the Sheffield Steelers over the wage capping violations and Sheffield were marked down to third place. Then in July it was reported that Cardiff had been fined £2,000 for refusing to release their books to the auditors. The wage capping rules were then amended for next year, the total salary cap would be £180,000 plus five cars and accommodation for five players.

The first year without Heineken sponsorship had turned out to be one full of drama both on and off the ice. With the first Chief Executive to guide the way forward maybe it was time for some major changes?

'I think the league needed some continuity with the rules regarding imports, wage capping and ice rink standards. Let's face it, some of those rinks we played in were death traps, it really is a wonder nobody was actually killed. The mesh around the boards definitely needed to be replaced with glass and the standards of dressing rooms were downright disgusting. It's a wonder rinks weren't shut down by health boards ... Durham, Teesside and the old Ayr rink for example.'

Despite a difficult year in Billingham, Todd Bidner re-signs for the Bombers for next season, hoping that the team would do better and encouraged by the signing of Chris Norton, André Malo and Richard LaPlante. Learning from last year, these players gave the Bombers a deadline of their own for sorting out the finances, after which they would look for another team. Although they hoped all would be well this would avoid them getting stuck in Teesside after the signing deadline day.

'All in all though, I had a great time in Britain. I played in a lot of great towns, met some wonderful people that I will always keep in touch with. I went back to University and received an Honours degree in Exercise Science, which I am very proud of.'

SEASON 1994/95
WITH
TONY HAND
BRITISH FORWARD FOR THE
EDINBURGH RACERS

	GP	G	A	Pts	PIM
PLAY-OFF CHAMPIONSHIP	6	9	15	24	10
PREMIER LEAGUE	44	72	150	222	44
BENSON & HEDGES CUP	11	12	24	36	20
TOTALS	61	93	189	282	74

PLAY-OFF CHAMPIONSHIPS: SHEFFIELD STEELERS

PREMIER DIVISION: SHEFFIELD STEELERS

BENSON & HEDGES CUP: NOTTINGHAM PANTHERS

Chapter Seven

So what did happen in Murrayfield at the end of last season? The Racers had first left the Murrayfield rink mid season, then returned after the BIHA brokered a deal, only to be chucked out before the play-offs had finished. Tony Hand explains:

> 'There was a problem with the rent. The consortium at that time, Bert Adams and Derek Reilly, had come to a disagreement with the rink regarding the rent. If you don't pay the rent you can't play, so we went and played in Livingston. It was funny because we went into the ice rink grabbed our equipment and went out the back door! It was ridiculous, really, to be honest. It was amateurish that it came to that, but the reality was that they had to pay the rent and they never paid it.'

In June the BIHA suspended Derek Reilly and Bert Adams from running the club as they continued to have substantial debts with the governing body (not least, one suspects, the £5,000 fine for breach of the wage capping regulations). What would this mean for the team and its loyal servant, best British Ice Hockey Player, Murrayfield's own Tony Hand?

In July the BIHA announce that Murrayfield Racers' place in the Premier Division will be taken by a new club, the Edinburgh Ice Hockey Club, which is run jointly by the rink and a group of local businessmen. One of the first players to sign for the new team? Tony Hand.

> 'They were looking for some of the senior players to sign because they didn't want to take over a team that wasn't there. They asked a few senior players to return, I negotiated with them, came to an agreement and decided to sign, and that encourages other players to join and attracts more people to the team in sponsors and what not. They wouldn't want to go into it with all the players leaving so that was one of the reasons. I felt a bit of a duty to sign right away, because of the fans, because it's my home town, I was happy to sign. I could have had more money elsewhere, but I decided to put my name to it and it kept the organisation going for another year.'

The Murrayfield Rink has a long history in British Ice Hockey. It was built in 1939 and then promptly requisitioned by the government for the war effort. It finally opened as an ice rink, with Sandy Archer as general manager in 1952. For the 52/53 season a new team, the Edinburgh Royals, joined the Scottish league. They went on to join the first British league for the 54/55 season but dropped out after one year. As Murrayfield Racers they competed from 1966 to 1982 in the Northern League and were again founder members of the second British League in 1982/83.

In the summer of 1994 Division One decides, just before the season begins, to restructure back into one unregionalised circuit. This means some 52 games need to be played, the longest British League Season ever, and eight more games than the Premiership. The BIHA bring out the new fixture list only 19 days before the first games are to be played!

Once again the season starts with the Benson and Hedges Cup first round played in four regionalised groups. Fife Flyers take Group A with the only maximum points, eight wins from eight games, Edinburgh Racers finish in second. Veteran (and sometimes Sky commentator) Bob Korol made his debut for Racers against Fife in the cup but could not stop his new team being beaten by 10-1.

In all the other groups the top two teams could only be separated by the number of goals scored. Group B Humberside Hawks and Durham Wasps finish with eleven points, and in Group C Nottingham and Sheffield finish with fourteen each. It is Sheffield who take the headlines with both regular netminders back-stopping shut-outs: they beat Romford Raiders 19-0 away (Martin Mckay between the pipes) and 13-0 at home (Andy Havenhand). The Steelers nearly shut-out Peterborough Pirates too, Martin Mckay only being beaten by Cam Plante 62 seconds from time. In Group D Cardiff and Slough are tied on twelve points pushing Basingstoke into third place.

On September 22nd the Durham Ice Rink was sold to Rex Brown, a local businessman. Three weeks later Incredo Ltd, the company that had controlled the Durham Wasps, went under to the tune of £440,000. Wasps continued the season under Rex Brown's control still based at the Durham rink.

From October 7th to the 9th Cardiff Devils are representing Great Britain in the European Cup quarter finals staged in Holland. The Devils first take on the Ukrainian Champions Sokol Kiev who had beaten them 9-1 in the same competition last year. This year was different. Cardiff took the first period 2-0, the second 3-0 and it was not until the first minute of the third period that the Ukrainians found a way past Stevie Lyle in the Cardiff net. Cardiff finished 6-2 winners and fourteen year old Stevie Lyle was destined to become a British Ice Hockey star. Then Cardiff took on Tilburg Trappers and lost 7-4. During the game Cardiff goalie Jason Wood is knocked unconscious by a slap shot from Trappers import, Kip Noble. Next up were the Champions of Kazakhstan Torpedo Ust-Kamenogorsk. To go through in second place Cardiff had to avoid being beaten by more than two goals. Hilton Ruggles scored after just 21 seconds, and by the start of the third period it was 3-3. Cardiff had taken many fans with them and when Ian Cooper backhanded the puck into the net with five minutes left on the clock, they went wild. Cardiff won this final game 4-3 and that meant they had won the group.

> 'That was brilliant, excellent. You look back and, at that time *in Europe we were such a small force. But that was a transition period with having more dual nationals on the team, more professionals. Cardiff when they went to Europe that year, everyone thought "they'll do all right but they'll be struggling." When they won it and got through I was as happy as anybody that they got through, a British team. They went to the next level and got beaten, because they'd gone up that next step, but it was such an achievement to be there.*'

October is also the month for the Quarter finals of the B&H Cup, played home and away. Edinburgh Racers take their revenge for the 10-1 defeat by Fife Flyers as they put out their Scottish rivals winning both games for a 13-10 overall score. Cardiff Devils dismiss the Durham Wasps 4-3 away and 15-2 at home. Nottingham Panthers put out Slough Jets and Sheffield Steelers defeat local rivals Humberside Hawks.

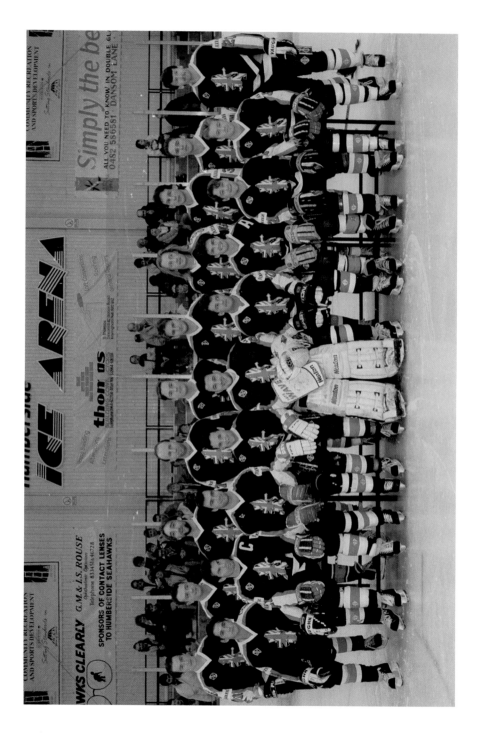

The Great Britain squad that won promotion from Pool C in Hull (1992)

The Great Britian squad watch as the Union Flag is raised after winning gold in Holland (1993) for promotion to Pool A

Great Britain v Canada - World Championship Pool A in 1994. Rick Brebant takes on a Canadian forward

Tony Hand in action for Great Britain

Ron Shudra and the Sheffield Steelers celebrate winning the
Premier League (1994/95)

Tony with brother Paul after Murrayfield win the 1993 Benson and Hedges Cup

Steve Lyle celebrates with Cardiff, Superleague Champions (1996/97)

Scott Young and Ayr winning Superleague (1997/98)

European Cup, Quarter Final Group A :	Tilburg, Netherlands						
	GP	W	L	D	GF	GA	Pts
Cardiff Devils	3	2	1	0	14	12	4
Torpedo Ust Kamenogorsk	3	2	1	0	14	12	4
Sokol Eskulap Kiev	3	1	2	0	13	14	2
Tilburg Trappers	3	1	2	0	12	18	2

On October 23rd in Durham Paul Hand of the Edinburgh Racers is told to take the early shower and is later banned for six games for his clash with Durham's Richard Little.

'When we went on the road ... we had quite a tough team and whenever there was trouble, all of a sudden there were four fights and it was our guys in the [penalty] box, and all of a sudden we had no players left. If we calmed down and kept out of the box we were fine! But we had too many guys who like the rough stuff, like Mike Ware, my brother Paul, Scott Plews, Ivan, but they were good players. We were all a lot younger then and we all used to get in trouble.'

The beginning of November sees the semi-finals of the Benson and Hedges Cup. Sheffield take on the Cardiff Devils and lose at home for the first time since December 27 the previous year. Cardiff win over the two legs 12-8.

Two days before Edinburgh take on Nottingham in the cup semis, Chris Palmer returns to the club.

'They got Chris [Palmer] back in. Me, Ivan [Matulik] and Chris just clicked.'

However they did not click in time for the Nottingham game, televised live on Sky Sports.

'Nineteen-two, I remember that. We went down there and we all just played the worst game we ever played in our lives. They just came out, and everything they did, they scored. We just played terrible. I remember we had a potential new sponsor on the bus. They came down with us to watch ice hockey, and us, for the first time and then we get beat nineteen-two. The new owners weren't too happy. Nottingham are always good in their own rink, and they were a good team, playing brilliantly, but seventeen difference!'

'We decided on the way back to play smart and win in Edinburgh. Blaisdell was going crazy because they like to win. The game meant nothing, Nottingham were through but they were playing brilliant then, and we did really well at home 9-6. We thought "How did we turn that seventeen goals round in one night?" We were quite happy with that.'

After Durham's poor show against Cardiff in the quarter final of the B&H Cup and with continuing poor form in the league, the new management of the Durham Wasps sacked coach Rocky Saganiuk and import Chris McKenzie. They appointed Richard Little as player coach.

On November 11th the Cardiff Devils became the first British club to take part in the semi-finals of the European cup. Having travelled to Minsk the Devils found the level somewhat higher than the quarter final, losing all three games 13-2, 14-0 and 13-1. They had signed ex-NHL Doug Smail, who played for Fife last year, on a short term contract to bolster the ranks. However they had also lost Stephen Cooper, Paul Heavey and James Manson to injury which tempted coach John Lawless back onto the ice, to no avail.

In Blackburn, their three imports decided to take to the ice after the game in … only their skates! They were later fired by Blackburn and the BIHA banned them from signing for another British club.

On November 13th it is Whitley Warriors turn to have disciplinary problems. Netminder Peter Graham is dismissed in their home game against Fife just days after their other goalie Kevin Dean had been thrown out of the game in Fife. Teenage goalie Tony McAleavy was thrown in at the deep end and despite having to have a cut stitched up during the game, helps Whitley to win 5-4. Kevin Dean is later banned for six games and Peter Graham until 23rd January.

The Teesside Bombers are desparately struggling and on November 27th they are beaten 14-0 at Medway. British defenceman Mark Pallister acts as Captain and finds fourteen players to get together and play the fixture, but Teesside are only able to ice one import for the game. The Medway fans show their appreciation of the effort and raise £300 to help pay for the coach trip. On the same night Whitley unveils its 'altuglass' down the sides of the rink. Whitley is the first of the North-Eastern teams to start replacing the netting round the rink.

December 3rd and the Sheffield Arena plays host to the final of the Benson and Hedges Cup between the Cardiff Devils and the Nottingham Panthers. A near capacity crowd of 8,000 saw Nottingham coach Mike Blaisdell lead the way on the ice as his side took the game with four unanswered goals in the middle period. The game finished 7-2 to Nottingham. The injury hit Devils had Jamie Van der Horst debut for them and he collected the Gold Award for their man of the match. Mike Blaisdell, who only iced because import Darren Schwartz quit the club at short notice, scored a hat trick and took the Gold Award for Man of the Match of his team.

> 'Mike has done well at Nottingham. He changed from player to coach and I always wondered why he had done it. He was still one of their better players, but I think he had a niggly back and that's why he changed to coaching. Obviously he has made the change with no problem at all, which doesn't always happen.'

The next night Nottingham play Cardiff, again, this time in the league, and drop their first point in thirteen league matches as they tie the game 6-6. Hilton Ruggles nearly won it for the beaten finalists when he hit the post with 13 seconds left on the clock.

On December 18th Edinburgh Racers travel to Whitley and chalk up a 13-2 road win. This game sees Tony become the first player ever to score 2,000 points in the British League (excluding play-off and cup games). He scored 3-5-8 in that game which took his totals after 423 games over 13 seasons to 840 goals -1166 assists -2006 points in total. The achievement is even more impressive when you consider that none of the other eleven players above 1,000 points are British born and trained.

'I don't think anyone else will achieve that, the way the game's gone. Edinburgh presented me with some prizes and I got some from the league. I was happy. You are always happy when you get a spot in the record books. In those days I never thought too much about it. These days it would have got a lot more coverage; it would have made a lot of the newspapers and even the television, but in them days it was only stats people and a few people who listen to the BIHA hotline who knew!'

Tony Hand in Edinburgh uniform

On December 26th Ken Priestlay made his debut for the Sheffield Steelers, at home to the Peterborough Pirates. The Steelers win 9-5 with Ken scoring 1+4. Ken Priestlay is one of the highest quality players to come to Britain in the modern era. Not only did he play in the NHL, he has two Stanley Cup rings from his time with the Pittsburgh Penguins.

'Kenny was an excellent addition to British Ice Hockey. He is probably one of the most professional players I have ever played with and I think Sheffield were very

lucky to get him. I knew when he came across he was on a different level from the league and I don't think Sheffield would have won the league without him.'

The next night there was extra seating installed at the Sheffield Arena for the Steelers game against local rivals Nottingham Panthers and this pushed the attendance record up to 9,270 people who saw a 3-3 draw.

December 31st sees Paul Hand return for Edinburgh. After he was banned for six games, he decided to make use of the enforced time off to have an operation on a damaged knee and this kept him out of the game until now. Also on 31st Cardiff won at home 17-5 over Bracknell and go unbeaten at home for two years!

The Lee Valley Lions have a way of making Teesside's struggles look tame. Without Lee Valley someone else would have to come bottom of Division One and so the BIHA always found a way of keeping them in the league. They are also known for having a small but fanatical band of supporters who are welcome wherever they travel in hockey land. On January 1st Lee Valley Lions owner/manager/coach/player/stick boy, Steve James, adds goalie to his list of duties when Mel Grundy is injured and there is no back-up on the bench. He faces 13 shots in 14.36 minutes allowing Guildford just two goals.

Teesside's troubles deepen on 9th January when chairman Dave Rennison resigns amid renewed doubts about the club's future. Many of the senior players have already found themselves new clubs. Valuable import defenceman Chris Norton who had joined the club for the new season and forward Todd Bidner who had stayed after a difficult season last year, find new jobs with nearby Durham Wasps.
Nottingham Panthers continue to do well as they take their unbeaten run to 20 games by beating Peterborough 13-6. Next up for Nottingham are the enemy up the road as they take on the Steelers in the House of Steel in front of another huge crowd. The unbeaten run comes to an end with a 9-8 win for the Steelers.

On the same night, Lee Valley Lions defeat Paisley Pirates 11-7 at home, one of the highlights of the year for Lee Valleys' band of devoted players and supporters.

Edinburgh Racers had signed Czech Stanko Horansky at the beginning of the season and he was popular with the Edinburgh crowd but failed to settle in and in January asked to be released.

'The hockey was maybe a bit better than Stan [Horansky] thought, and he never settled: his wife was home sick and they didn't speak too much English. It was tough for him so the club released him.'

Three days later the BIHA announced that luckless Teesside Bombers were to withdraw from the league due to mounting financial problems. With the signing deadline rapidly approaching, the remaining players at Teesside were quickly finding new teams to play for and with Horansky gone, Edinburgh sign up Merv Priest from the hapless Bombers.

'Cleveland were never going to survive in their ice rink. It was part of a complex, swimming and skating, etc. I don't know if it is still the same in the lower division, but in many rinks there was no toilet in the changing rooms. So you go to the toilet in the game and you are standing there with all your equipment on and there is a fan standing next to you, and usually they would start shouting at you in the toilets because there were no stewards. That's not very professional. The facility at Billingham [spectator capacity of 1,200] was just never going to allow you to run a viable team.'

On January 22nd Edinburgh Racers were back in Whitley Bay. Back between the pipes for Whitley was Kevin Dean, but not for long!

'Whitley Bay was famous for high scoring games. They once had one of their regular goalies out and then Kevin Dean gets thrown out so they put one of their imports, Dean Richards, in the net and he did a better job!!! They were always offensive, high scoring games at Whitley.'

When Kevin Dean is dismissed from the game, Tony McAleavy is again the young replacement, but this time he conceded eleven goals from 19 shots, so for the third period Dean Richards goes between the pipes and saves 14 out of the 19 shots he faces. However the change of netminder is too late to stop Edinburgh taking the game 16-10.

On January 27th Team Canada come to Britain and kick-off a short tour in Peterborough. A strengthened Peterborough side achieve the unthinkable and win 3-2.

'We played against them [Team Canada] at Paisley. We played against Chris [Palmer], he knew the coaches, but they had brought across college guys, it wasn't really proper Team Canada. There is no way that the real Team Canada would get beat at Peterborough. They came across to see how the young guys played, they weren't interested in hammering anybody.'

Stevie Lyle has been playing well for the Cardiff Devils alongside Jason Woods, then against Peterborough on the 29th he was between the pipes for Cardiff's 9-0 win.

'It is an excellent achievement for any fifteen year old to be playing at that level and then to get a shut-out. I think for him to record a shut-out regardless of whether it was an easy game or a hard game, it was still an amazing achievement, and Stevie should be happy that he has set a few records. The way things are going, there aren't going to be any British goalies coming through. Its an excellent achievement.'

At the beginning of February the BIHA announce the appointment of George Peternousek, former Durham Wasps coach, as coach of the GB team. Both coach Alex Dampier and assistant coach Peter Johnson had resigned earlier in the year. Both stated that their resignations had nothing to do with the fact that this year the Wembley final weekend clashed with the World Championship Pool B!

'That was ridiculous, it just wouldn't happen anywhere else. You couldn't have any training camps, it was a case of whoever can, just go play.'

Nottingham's run of form looked a little shaky as they lost in Durham and drew with ninth placed Peterborough Pirates.

'I can't remember what happened to them but in those days you only needed one or two key players out and you would lose. It was really that straightforward. It was so tough for teams, and I think Nottingham had a few injuries.'

At the Peterborough game, coach Mike Blaisdell's desire to win bubbled over into a fit of temper, firstly verbally abusing ref Ken Taggart and then squirting him with water. Apparently, having been chucked out of the game for this Mike then kicked a door off its hinges, just for good measure. Blaisdell was fined £250 and asked to issue an apology for his actions and his reported post match comments. The team were also fined for leaving the ice at the end of the game before the post match presentations.

If you think Mike's behaviour was a little bizarre, on February 11th, referee Steve Harber was caught on camera climbing the plexi-glass at Telford to hit a supporter who had leaned over and hit him! A similar incident occurred involving England's chief referee Bob Bramah but after rink management admitted that the supporter was a known trouble maker no action was taken against ref Bramah, whilst ref Harber was reinstated after a two weeks absence.

With the title chase getting closer between Nottingham, Cardiff and Sheffield, Cardiff lose points at Durham at the end of February. March kicks off with Cardiff at home to the Sheffield Steelers and Sheffield take the first away victory there since January 1993 with a 3-4 win. Tommy Plommer scored the game winning goal with just 1.31 left on the clock. The battle is now between the Steelers and the Panthers for top spot.

'That was certainly the start of the more professional leagues. They [Cardiff, Nottingham, Sheffield] didn't just want four or five full timers, they were wanting a team of full timers, and if they had the finance they were well within their rights to do it. Teams like Sheffield, Cardiff and Nottingham took the league forward. The league had to make a decision about which way it was going to go, either stagnate or let the other teams come in who had more resources, more fans, better facilities, and try to bring hockey on. Obviously they made the right decision.'

On March 13th the BIHA announced that the top four Premier clubs and Division One Guildford have breached the wage capping regulations. This would mean a £5000 fine and five points deducted. However within a week all the clubs had been cleared, the accountants admitted to making an error in the case of Edinburgh and the other clubs were cleared on appeal.

Having covered the Benson and Hedges tournament this year, Sky TV announced in March that it would be covering British Ice Hockey for at least the next three years, starting with 1995/96 season.

On the last weekend of the league season, Sheffield Steelers win their first Premier Division title, when they win 8-6 in Nottingham. The Nottingham Ice Rink is full to capacity with over 3,000 fans present, but few Steelers fans have been able to get tickets. The Steelers set up a live transmission back in the Ponds Forge sports complex in Sheffield so another 2,000 fans can watch the game on a giant TV screen. Ken Priestlay shows his class, leading by example as he scores five of the goals. When the Steelers team return to the Arena, the fans are there in large numbers to greet their heroes.

'When we came back after Wembley [96/97] it was an excellent feeling to see all the fans. So I can imagine what it was like back then in 95/96 - that first time after the Nottingham game, you really started to feel like superstars when you came back to that.'

The next night, the last night of the regular season, Sheffield travel to Durham slightly hungover from the previous evening's events and Durham take full advantage winning easily over the new League Champions. Nottingham travel to Cardiff and finish their season with a bench clearance. A total of ten players were dismissed from the game and referee John Moore handed out 285 minutes in penalties. Both teams were fined £2500 for the incident but apart from Brian Cox, netminder for Nottingham, most players did not receive lengthy bans.

'The teams had to play at Wembley so they couldn't give anyone any big suspensions or there would have been no-one there. To me that was amateurish, but the sport came first.'

Top of the scoring chart for the Premier League is Tony with 207 points (and 28 penalty minutes) In second is line mate Ivan Matulik with 167 points (and 93 penalty minutes). Peterborough's outstanding Randy Smith was in third, pushing Chris Palmer, the third member of Edinburgh's first line, into fourth with 162 points (and 55 penalty minutes).

British League Premier Division	GP	W	L	D	GF	GA	Pts
Sheffield Steelers	44	35	5	4	334	183	74
Cardiff Devils	44	32	8	4	366	217	68
Nottingham Panthers	44	32	8	4	372	213	68
Edinburgh Racers	44	25	14	5	335	289	55
Durham Wasps	44	22	19	3	264	242	47
Fife Flyers	44	20	20	4	271	242	42
Basingstoke Beavers	44	20	22	2	271	279	42
Humberside Hawks	44	17	21	6	331	330	40
Peterborough Pirates	44	12	27	5	248	368	29
Whitley Warriors	44	10	30	4	242	372	24
Milton Keynes Kings	44	9	31	4	248	363	22
Bracknell Bees	44	6	35	3	189	373	15

The position of teams tied on points was decided on the results of games between them

'That was a great line. I liked playing alongside Ivan. Ivan liked to skate. Ivan didn't want the puck until you gave it to him and I prefer a player like that. Just wait until he gets his speed up and then pass to him and he'd get so many chances. I think my absolute favourite player to play with is Ed Courtenay [Sheffield 97/98]. The league will be lucky to see another player like Ed.'

The top four teams are in the bottom half of the table when it comes to the fair play award. Fife Flyers are top of that table with 557 penalty Minutes (Pims) an average of 12.6 per game, whilst Whitley Warriors and their goalie problems are bottom with 1177 Pims an average of 26.7. Nottingham 25.4 average and Sheffield 21.8 average complete the bottom end of this table.

Edinburgh's season had seen just nine victories out of 22 away fixtures.

'We still took the hockey very seriously. It wasn't just a laugh, we had a lot of winners in the team and we were all desperate to win, we loved winning. But we had such a small squad you couldn't go home worrying about a loss. A lot of times we were just beaten by exhaustion, it sounds ridiculous, but the first game on the road we had a chance of winning but the second game we were just so tired, its no excuse, its just that is really how it was. We (me, Ivan and Chris) were one of the best lines in the league, and we had good defence but we just didn't have enough, we just ran out of players. And if anyone got injured or suspended (suspensions were longer in those days) that was it.'

For the Wembley play-offs Group A consisted of last year's Champs, Cardiff Devils, with Edinburgh Racers, Basingstoke Beavers and Durham Wasps. Despite their end of season win over the Steelers, Durham finished bottom of the group without a win at all. Basingstoke also failed to make it to the Championship final, despite the return of coach Peter Woods, replacing Gary Douville for the play-offs.

In Group B nothing was decided until the last weekend of games, Fife and Humberside battling hard with Nottingham and Sheffield. Sheffield played their first three games away, losing twice with both Ron Shudra and Steve Nemeth out injured. They return to the Arena and win all their home games to finish top of the group. A total of 24,212 watched those three games at the Arena.

In the promotion/relegation games the Division One teams opened the campaign by beating their Premiership rivals. Swindon Wildcats beat Whitley Warriors 10-7, Paisley Pirates beat the Bracknell Bees 5-2 and Telford Tigers beat Milton Keynes Kings 5-3.

'That's very unusual. Sometimes winning teams keep winning and losing teams lose it and panic a little bit, but in those days I cannot stress too much how injuries and suspensions had such an impact on how the games went. If you had a better player injured or suspended after Christmas you could lose the league. Nowadays teams are better able to cope with it.'

The top four teams in Division One joined the bottom four from the Premier to play-off for the right to play in the Premiership next year. The league was being restructured down to ten teams in each of three divisions so there are only two slots in the Premier to battle for this year.

In Group A it went right down to the wire, and in their last game Slough faced-off an hour later than Peterborough Pirates so they knew they had to score nine goals more than their opposition to go up. The celebrations were in Slough when Darren Zinger scored in the last minute to take the game to 14-5 and take Slough into the Premier. Peterborough were left to ponder the implications of that hour's difference in face-off times.

The other group saw Whitley Warriors hold on to their Premier place whilst Milton Keynes Kings were relegated after just one year in the top flight. On April 9th Whitley fans did not get the party night they anticipated as the last game of the season against Swindon was called to a halt at 35.03, with Warriors leading 3-1, by referee George Nicholson. The Zamboni (which resurfaces the ice) had broken down and the ice surface was unplayable. The party turned into an angry protest instead.

On April 12th Great Britain open their World Championship campaign with a 7-3 defeat against host nation Slovakia. Next day they took on Romania and lost 2-0. Romania failed to beat anybody else and were later relegated to Pool C. The GB team had unwisely run themselves ragged trying to beat the Slovakia team who were later promoted, leaving themselves tired for a game that they should have won.

Three of the team, Captain Shannon Hope, Nicky Chinn and Ashley Tait then fly back to the UK to play for their club teams in the Wembley finals over the weekend.

The first Semi final, on Saturday 15th April brings last year's finalists together, as the Cardiff Devils take on the Sheffield Steelers. It was one of the best games the Wembley finals has ever seen. Cardiff took a 2-0 lead after four minutes, but there was no thought of last years defeat as Steelers fought back with two goals to finish the first period tied on 2-2. Sheffield took the lead after 1.36 of the second period but this time Cardiff came back with a goal at 14.28. In the third period it was Cardiff's turn to take the lead but Ken Priestlay scored the equaliser for the Steelers. The sixty minutes finished tied at 4-4. Neither side could find the back of the net in overtime, taking it to penalty shots. Sheffield took the penalty shots 3-1 and were through to the final.

The second semi saw the Edinburgh Racers take on the Nottingham Panthers. This was going to be no repeat of the 19-2 thrashing earlier in the year. In contrast to the tight game earlier in the day this was a wide open offensive game of hockey. The Racers were the first on the score board after 3.17 and had three by 13.17. Nottingham pulled it back to 2-3 before the first break. The second period was tied 3-3. In the third Edinburgh just extend their lead with a 2-5 period to take the game 7-11.

'That was probably the best game we played all year. We knew when we won it, it sounds harsh, but we knew when we won it we would struggle the next day, after playing the night game. They'd [Sheffield] had two meals by the time we had got off the ice.'

Whilst the top four club teams are battling it out at Wembley, GB take on the Netherlands and win 3-2 .

On the morning of the Championship Final, Fife Flames and Durham Mosquitoes Junior C (16 and under) teams met for the third time in five years in the British Junior C Championship. Flames took the first encounter in 1992 and Durham took the second in 1993.

British Junior C Championship
Wembley Arena 16th April

Fife Flames 5   Durham Mosquitoes.......1   (0-1, 0-0, 0-1 OT 0-0)
Fife Scorers: Petrie 2+1, Venter 1+2, Finaly 1+1, Mercer 1g,
Durham Scorers: McDonough 1g, Hillier 1a

The Championship Final faced off on Sunday 16th April and any chance the tired Racers had was not helped by playing much of the first ten minutes short-handed, penalty killing. Referee for the game was Graham Horner with Linesmen Alan Craig and Andy Carson. After the penalties calmed down, Sheffield took a two goal lead going into the first break. Edinburgh pulled it back to 2-2 at the beginning of the second but back came Sheffield to draw the second period 2-2. In the third Edinburgh ran out of gas and the Steelers took the period 3-0 and the game 7-2.

This was the Racers fifth Championship defeat in six appearances, but after the troubles the club had gone through at the beginning of the season and the strength of the teams they faced, being in the final was a major achievement in itself.

> *'An excellent year, a great bunch of guys. One of the best years I've had at ice hockey, just actual enjoyment, being in the dressing room, being on the bus with the guys, great bunch of guys. Ivan Matulik, Mike [Ware], Dean Edmiston, its one of these seasons you really look back on, when you're forty years on, its going to be one of the ones you remember. Obviously you were a professional player, but you were enjoying yourself too. There were only three or four of us who never went to work, the rest of the guys had to sacrifice a lot of time with wives, girlfriends and families for ice hockey, but they enjoyed it as well. Just the banter around, in those days the last thing we talked about in the dressing room was ice hockey. You play in a lot of teams, with that many people coming and going, you don't really keep in touch, but this team, in this season … We went all the way to the final at Wembley with such a few guys, that was unbelievable, we never won anything but for us personally we had a very successful year.'*

Meanwhile, back in Bratislava, the GB team are taking on Denmark, and losing 9-2. Man of the match for GB was a young man from Whitley Bay called David Longstaff. At the end of the Championships he had picked up another man of the match award and was Best British forward selected by the organisers.

Nicky Chinn returned to the GB team having picked up a limp, Ashley Tait did not return at all having broken his leg! On Tuesday a jaded GB side were beaten by a 53rd

Chapter Eight

So much happened in the world of British Ice Hockey this year, both on and off the ice that it's going to be really difficult to fit it all in. To start with there were two new arenas; one in Manchester sporting an all new ice hockey team, called the Storm, and one in Newcastle adopting the Whitley Warriors who now became the Newcastle Warriors. But that is not all, the Durham Wasps team had been sold in the summer to Sir John Hall but the Durham rink was still owned by Rex Brown (*and that is the short version*). So Sir John Hall got permission from the BIHA to play his team, still called the Durham Wasps, from Sunderland leisure centre: whilst the die hard Durham fans formed the Durham *City* Wasps playing in the English League and made 'T'-shirts warning against 'expensive imitations'. Chris Norton had played for the Durham Wasps under rink owner Rex Brown in 1994/95 but for this season was signed to the Newcastle/Whitley Warriors. So are you sitting comfortably? Then we'll begin.

Chris Norton came to this country to play for the Ayr Raiders. His first experience of Whitley Warriors was playing against them in the quarter finals of the B&H Cup, he got hit into the boards during the play and a supporter kicked him! - a far cry from his early professional career as an ice hockey player. He was drafted by the Winnipeg Jets and spent three seasons in their minor league set up. He was traded to Chicago Blackhawks and then on to Los Angeles where he was playing with the Phoenix Roadrunners and met a man called Brent Sapergia who said that with Chris's British relatives he could probably get a good job in the UK. Despite all his grandparents and his mother being British, Chris could not get a British passport at that time, because his father is not British and that was all that counted.

In July 95 the Premier clubs agree to a salary cap of £250,000.

> *'In principle I think it was a good idea. I know that they have used it successfully in the NBA [National Basketball Association] in North America, and it has worked quite well, but in order for it to work well it needs to be policed well. You need to have people who are monitoring how much money guys are being paid and all the other things right from the word go. Its like saying the speed limit along here is seventy miles an hour but if you never have a policeman along here, who is going to watch it? And I think that was one of the problems. In principle I think its a good idea because it creates a level playing field for your Bracknells and Basingstokes, but other people say why hurt the teams that go out and create fan interest. Yeah, they've got big arenas but they've still got to fill those big arenas.'*

The BIHA were also persuaded by the teams to allow any player who can get a British passport to play as British, and play on the GB team regardless of where he learnt his sport. It then transpires that a player who has *never held a Canadian passport* and can show some form of British ancestry, can claim a British passport. The stampede to sign such players begins, even though the standard of some is questionable. There is the added bonus that there is no transfer fee for these adopted Brits as there is for good British born and trained players already in the league.

The Season starts with the Autumn Cup first round, again sponsored by Benson & Hedges this year. Newcastle Warriors are still playing in Whitley Bay and Manchester Storm's first home game is held at ... Milton Keynes. The Manchester Storm are led by the man who made it happen for Cardiff, John Lawless. As Sheffield had done, Manchester develop a bunch of nicknames for their players. There can be only one for the bench coach who just can't help stepping on to the ice, so it becomes John 'Boomerang' Lawless. John had brought Daryl Lypsey from Swindon as a player and his assistant coach. He also brought Hilton Ruggles with him from Cardiff. Lawless leaving Cardiff opened the door for Paul Heavey to take on the role of coach for the Devils. Heavey has signed Mike Ware and Ivan Matulik from Edinburgh and last year's player of the year, Randy Smith, from Peterborough as his imports and everyone expects Cardiff to do well, despite being "Lawless".

Manchester's first home game in the new Nynex arena takes place on 15th September in the B&H cup against Telford Tigers. After announcing that anyone wearing a British League replica shirt could get in for £1, the 10,034 attendance comes close to breaking the mythical British attendance record. The Nynex Arena was built as part of the Manchester dream of hosting the 2000 Olympics after their bid for the '96 failed. Unfortunately for the Olympic bid team, the Nynex didn't swing the odds in their favour, but it gave the people of Manchester a multi-million pound 17,000 seat arena. To make such a venue viable on a week to week basis needs more than major rock and pop concerts, it needs sport, and the Arena quickly became home to both the Manchester Giants basketball team and ice hockey's Storm.

Manchester started in ice hockey as far back as 1910 when the Manchester Ice Palace opened. By 1913 they were using that well known hockey slogan 'the fastest game on earth'. After the First World War, Manchester was the only rink in England staging Ice Hockey for eight years. Equipment was makeshift with football shin pads and a stout pair of gloves comprising the protective kit. After the Second World War the Ice Palace once again returned to business but this time without ice hockey and it finally shut its doors in April 1967.

In 1995 at the end of the first round of the B&H Cup, Fife Flyers top Group A, with Newcastle Warriors runners up. In Group B Durham Wasps took the top spot with Humberside in second, the newly formed Manchester Storm propped up the bottom of this group. Group C went to Sheffield with arch rivals Nottingham Panthers second. Finally top of Group D was Cardiff Devils with the Basingstoke Bison behind them. These teams went into home and away quarter finals; Sheffield beat Cardiff, Nottingham beat Basingstoke, Fife put out Newcastle and Humberside beat Durham.

As the league gets underway things do not go well for Newcastle Warriors. They are thrashed by local rivals Durham 12-1 and this brings the sacking of coach Terry Matthews.

'Terry Matthews is a tremendous man, a great guy, he really is, but he was thrown into a bad situation from the get go. We had a team that could not come close to competing in that league at the time, and we lost. We just did not have the horses, and for some reason Francis Smith [owner of the Warriors] thought that

the way to turn this around was to get rid of Terry. I disagreed with that, and he asked me "Will you do it for a few games until we replace you with someone else?" Well that's fine, but player coach is not possible, it really isn't. And then Garry [Douville] comes in and at that point I think Francis opened up the wallet a little and allowed him to bring some more players in and for that reason we started to win a few more games. I don't think it had anything to do with Garry Douville's coaching whatsoever.'

The end of October, beginning of November sees the semi-finals of the B&H Cup. Sheffield stumble, going down 3-5 in Fife but come back to win 6-3 in the home leg. The home leg sees new netminder Wayne Cowley making his debut for Sheffield and Tony Hand scores a beauty for his new team in sudden death overtime. Nottingham put out Humberside 16-8 on aggregate.

On 9th November Manchester Storm, whose league form had picked up since the B&H Cup, were at home against local rivals Blackburn Hawks, live on Sky TV and in front of 8,975 fans. They lost their discipline and then the game losing 9-12. Teams weren't supposed to travel to an arena like Manchester and win. Blackburn reminded the Storm that it wasn't the nice new venue that needed to play the ice hockey!

The first game in the Newcastle Arena takes place on 19th November against the Fife Flyers, in front of 4,089 fans. The Newcastle Arena is a valuable addition to ice hockey venues, but is more like the arenas built in the 80s' (Blackburn etc) than Sheffield or Manchester. There is one tier of seating with a 7,000 capacity for ice hockey, considerably less than at Manchester but still many more than the 3,200 at the old Whitley rink. At this stage Chris is acting as coach after Terry Matthews left and before Garry Douville who had been sacked from Telford earlier in the year is brought in as his replacement. The Flyers are first to score in the new building, and go on to win 6-4.

'I remember pretty well it was a strange night, just because. ... seeing all those Whitley Bay people I used to see at Hillheads sitting right on top of you, spread out in the crowd and you're like "jeez this is probably 'the changing of the guard' here as far as ice hockey goes in this country." In 95/96 it was still in reality a 'ma & pa business'. In Durham, Whitley Bay, or Fife it's been in the family or it's a town run thing. Creating national exposure was not on any of the minds of the people at that time. It was basically fill your little rink and you're happy.'

At the end of November Newcastle bring in Garry Douville.

'We got some new blood. That's all it was, we started getting the horses. We had a problem with one of the imports, Jason Smart, who they sacked. He didn't really settle in. There are a lot of good players that have come over here and haven't made it. They look at the statistics back in the leagues in Canada and they're tearing it up, "jeez that must be an awful - league he couldn't even play here." Well its a different brand of hockey here. Even at the beginning of that year, imports had to be able to do everything. You had to be able to carry the puck, you had to be able to shoot, you had to be able to score, you had to be able to play physical, you had to be able to ... If you didn't have some of those

attributes, or weren't used to it, you were history. So Smarty was gone. That hurt and we had to find someone else and another Finnish kid came over and it was really a long process getting this team to gel.'

The final of the B&H cup was held on 2nd December between the Nottingham Panthers and Sheffield Steelers. The Steelers played newly arrived Wayne Cowley in the net ahead of Marty Mckay who had been back stopping the Steelers on his own early in the season. Alex Dampier said it was the toughest decision he ever had to make. With the influx of "British" Canadians, many said this was a sign of the imminent death of the British player.

'With Mckay and Cowley there is no comparison of the two. Marty got them there and that's fine, but its a business and the business is winning and what you have to do is put the best possible team on the ice that you can, regardless of their accent, of their colour, of their size. Alex says, "its the hardest decision I ever had to make", well yeah OK it might be a difficult decision to make, but hey, with all respect to Marty because he is a good goalie and at that time he was a real good goalie, but there is no decision there, you go with Cowley, he's a better goalie plain and simple, who has NHL experience, whose got American Hockey League Championship experience, you do that.

Now that decision for me would be an easy one. On the other side there are the fringe Canadian players, the guys who have a British passport but never really played at a high level in North America, who maybe played in some sunshine Florida league or something like that and they are taking the place of some British players, like Ashley Tait who I think is a pretty good hockey player, and these guys are coming over and taking their jobs. Now I think there is a problem there, I definitely do, and that's where when they say "we don't have the right accent", I can't say I disagree with that. There is a worrying trend as far as the possibility of the British getting the chance to play, there are some decent ones who, given the chance, given the coaching, could contribute. But again every other team is stuffed full of Canadians or Europeans. We don't have the time to risk letting this kid get his feet wet by playing a few shifts a game when he might cost us and that's what the bottom line is.'

In the B&H final with Cowley between the pipes the Steelers took the first period 1-0, then broke away with three unanswered goals in the second period. The third period saw Nottingham fighting back with Durdle and Blaisdell scoring but Tony Hand sealed their fate with an empty net goal at 19.11. Sheffield had the first trophy of the season in the bag. With additional seating added, the capacity of the Sheffield Arena was increased to 10,142 and all the tickets were sold. The official attendance for the game was 10,136.

December 16th 1995 is a date that may stay with Steelers' Nicky Chinn longer than the B&H final, and no doubt with Ross Lambert too. In an incident behind the run of play, Ross Lambert receives a stick injury to his face and eye which requires 17 stitches. Emotions run high and result in a major brawl on the ice. The wisdom of letting a professional team play out of the Sunderland venue is brought into question when tempers flair in the corridors between Durham players and Sheffield fans. Nicky Chinn is questioned by police after the game. In the aftermath Chinn is suspended for three games, which again incenses Ross Lambert who begins legal proceedings against Chinn.

'The league really, really, blew that whole situation. They turned it in to a circus. They didn't take a stand, they didn't institute any authority whatsoever. For a lot of players, myself included, they finally confirmed what I'd always thought - that they were a bunch of people running scared. It hurt the game of hockey incredibly, the exposure that it got from that incident.

I wasn't on the team but I have played with the guys involved and talked about it and listened to it. The only reason that Ross took Nicky Chinn to court was the league did nothing to discipline this player. Rick Brebant cross-checks Gary Stefan in Slough and gets twelve or thirteen games, he cross-checked him. Nicky Chinn sticks Ross Lambert in the face, and gets three games. I am not in favour of guys taking other players to court, but I understand why Ross did it. At first I said, "that's garbage , there is no way a player should". But then you start hearing what happened and then what the league does about it, then you say "go, do it."'

In December the Jean-Marc Bosman rulings are ratified by the European court. Any EEC national should be able to work in any other EEC nation without restriction. This means that as well as being able to sign as many British passport holding Canadians as they like, teams can now sign as many European passport holders as they like. Durham move quickly to sign three Finnish born and trained players. Canadians with any European passport now become of interest and Milton Keynes sign Dutch-Canadian defender Phil Valk.

'I know Garry and Francis went after a couple and brought two Swedes in, who helped, but again it was getting the bodies in, guys who could play, not (in all fairness to those guys) not eighteen or nineteen year old British guys who had never really played at that level before, which is what we had for a while. We had kids out there playing, against former NHL hockey players, who had never played at a senior level before or maybe a handful of games and we just couldn't compete. It was a nightmare. There were some games when me and Steve Brown just looked at each other and went "this is going to be the longest season ever". You could see it coming, right at the beginning, you could see it, you could look at the schedule and say "we are just not going to beat any of these teams." Its so discouraging.'

The biggest crowd of the season at the Newcastle Arena (5,127) were there on 20th January to see the Warriors draw 3-3 with the Cardiff Devils.

'I remember that game, because I had broken a bone in my foot on 24th December in a five o'clock game against Basingstoke. I got hit with the puck and because the boot was so tight I didn't really notice until after the game and the next morning it had blown up. So I was out for two and a half weeks and my first game back was that Cardiff game. We were under-staffed that game too, we really were, but it was just one of those nights. I think Cardiff came in thinking they

were going to walk all over us, and we played a real good game and I remember Scotty Morrison got a short handed goal to tie it up three all and we held on. The team were starting to come together. Rick Fera joined the club, he was in the twilight of his career but he was a smart player. He wasn't going to score five goals a game like he used to because the game was much better, but he knew where to be, especially in the defensive zone, he wasn't a liability and that makes a big difference. The fans saw we were making inroads. While they weren't huge, we were slowly starting to be respectable and compete every night. The fans in the North East, they love a winner, they really do, but if they come to the match and see you are busting your ass every night and giving 110%, and you are out there playing for your club, then they are not overjoyed you are losing, but they are going to come back, because the effort is there.'

Chris Norton in action for Newcastle Warriors

Five days before the 31 January deadline, there is another big shake-up at struggling Newcastle which sees David Longstaff and recent recruit Tim Salmon cut and two Swedish players signed. The Warriors were later fined 2,000 Swiss francs (roughly £1,300) for playing Niklas Gulliksson and Lars Thunell without a release from the Swedish Federation. Scott Campbell a British Canadian was also signed to strengthen the blue line. Of all the changes the cutting of David Longstaff seemed like the worst thing to do, for Newcastle Warriors to sack their best British player, but with the number of foreigners now available, the future could have been bleak for Longstaff.

'In reality it was absolutely the best possible thing for David Longstaff to get out of Whitley Bay, without a doubt, the best possible thing. He was the glamour boy, a tremendous talent. He was excellent, and the best thing for Lobby was to get out of the atmosphere here, of knowing that no-one could touch him, that what he said went. Basically if the coach said "skate harder" he could look at him and laugh and say "yeah, right, whatever". That isn't a reflection of his attitude, that's just a young kid who has always been in the Whitley Bay system, who has always been the best. That's immaturity as an athlete and what he needed was to take that next step, move to a different organisation where there are coaches ... where basically, if he doesn't do what they say, he is going to sit on the bench and there are not going to be four thousand people in the crowd screaming for the coach's head because Longstaff is not playing.'

David now is, in my mind, not just one of the best British players but one of the best players in the league, because of his move to Sheffield, because he is playing with a group of players who don't know the David Longstaff of Whitley Bay. All the British guys there would look at Lobby and say "God he's good", but now he is playing with guys who are as good as him and don't know about his past history and don't stand back in awe and say "that's David Longstaff - you can't tell him to work harder."

I remember saying to myself then, this is going to be the making of this guy as a hockey player, he could have stayed in Whitley Bay and become stagnant and he could have just died there. Maybe he didn't want it, but he got a kick in the butt, mainly a personality conflict between him and Garry, but David Longstaff is playing for the [96/97] British Champions, and Garry Douville is where?'

On the 31st of January a meeting of the British League clubs hear proposals from Ice Hockey Superleague Ltd (ISL) on the formation of a new league for season 96/97.The proposal is for a franchise system with no promotion or relegation. Each club would have to show a certain level of financial security and a certain standard of facilities is required too. The major movers appear to be Sir John Hall, owner of the Durham Wasps, and George Dodds, who has taken over the running of Sheffield Steelers from Gardner-Brown. Clubs wishing to take part have to have a seating capacity of 2,000 in the first year going up to 5,000 in year five, not to mention lighting to TV standard and a budget for 17 professional players. Some heralded this as the brightest future ice hockey could possibly have. Others were worried and likened it to the first British League which had folded due to the high cost of a truly professional outfit.

With deadline day fast approaching there is the usual rash of last minute signings. On February 3rd Roger Hunt returned to Edinburgh and played for Murrayfield Royals against Swindon. He had been involved in a nasty incident in 1992 which saw Bracknell's import Lee Odelien hospitalised and both Hunt and Murrayfield's coach Koopmans were issued with life bans by the BIHA (see Chapter Four). At the time Roger had been charged with causing grievous bodily harm, but after the hearing had been delayed twice he returned to Canada and the case was left open. After playing three games for the Royals on his return, the Bracknell police come calling, Hunt appeared in court two days later, a fine was paid, and the matter was finally finished with.

Manchester Storm sign a British talent who goes by the name of Pallister. Mark Pallister, cousin of Manchester United footballer Gary Pallister. Although the Storm have defencemen out injured, some said it was a PR signing.

> *'Pally is a decent player, Pally's not a Superleague player and he knows that. He could be if he was coached properly, but he has never been coached. The biggest influence on his career has been André Malo, when they played in Billingham together, and I think he learnt all his hockey from André but you need a coach to teach you to play the game properly. There are a lot of British guys who could play in the Superleague, but they were never taught to play the game. So while their skill level is high, people say "wow he's a fast skater, he can shoot," well that's fine, but if he doesn't know where to be and he doesn't know how to play the defensive zone properly it doesn't matter because you are going to get beat. I think Pally falls into that category a little bit. He is a big strong tough kid who is a good skater for his size, but I just think he lacks the knowledge of the game a little bit to play at this level. Credit to André because he taught him a lot, but if someone had got a hold of him a few years back and taught him properly he could have played at the Superleague level. As far as signing him because of his cousin, well that was a brand new team and if it sells tickets, it sells tickets, nothing wrong with that, its marketing, you have got to get people in the door.'*

Mark's first game for the Storm is away at Medway, then the next night in front of 12,386 Storm fans he makes his home debut at the Storm Shelter against the Bracknell Bees.

On February 18th Manchester win Division One with a victory over Chelmsford, their 28th straight win, and with six games to spare. On Wednesday 21st 16,280 attend the midweek game at the Nynex to celebrate their Championship as the team take on season long rivals Blackburn. This time the score goes the right way for Manchester as they take the game 11-3.

Newcastle's season has taken a turn for the better with a draw at home to championship hopefuls Cardiff and a win at Nottingham in the Lace City. Best of all for the fans was the 5-5 draw at the House of Steel when Warriors were leading going into the last 2 minutes, then Tim Cranston saved the day for the Steelers with a late equaliser. Two wins over Milton Keynes Kings pulls Newcastle into eighth spot and a place in the Wembley Play-offs.

Manchester Storm celebrate winning Division One

Cardiff seem intent on giving the League to the Steelers, losing three games in a row through February, and on 28th the Steelers clinch the title in a 7-2 victory over the old enemy Nottingham Panthers, but unlike last year when the deciding game was in Nottingham, this year 9,246 fans are able to watch the game in the Sheffield Arena.

British League Premier Division	GP	W	L	D	GF	GA	Pts
Sheffield Steelers	36	27	4	5	268	122	59
Cardiff Devils	36	26	7	3	271	140	55
Durham Wasps	36	22	10	4	213	158	48
Nottingham Panthers	36	19	12	5	214	174	43
Humberside Hawks	36	16	16	4	202	235	36
Fife Flyers	36	14	16	6	209	238	34
Basingstoke Bison	36	11	20	5	146	190	27
Newcastle Warriors	36	10	22	4	167	256	24
Milton Keynes Kings	36	7	22	7	186	237	21
Slough Jets	36	5	28	3	172	298	13

Top of the League's scorers (with 46 goals and 77 assists for 123 points) and Player's Player of the Year both go to Tony Hand now of the Sheffield Steelers. Coach of the Year goes to Cardiff's Paul Heavey. Drew Fraser is awarded the Mick Curry Memorial Trophy for most improved Official.

On the 5th March Humberside sack John Griffiths and bring in Keith Milhench formerly of Bracknell to take them through the play-offs. On 9th the play-offs get off to a bad start for Hockey. Durham and Humberside meet in Sunderland and fights break out in

1995/96

warm-up due to ill feeling between former Durham player, Bruce Bell and his ex player coach Rick Brebant. Bruce Bell was taken to hospital and although order was restored and the game started, the police had been called and they ordered the referee to stop the game after 58 seconds. Various players were arrested, Lambert and Weaver faced assault charges, but they were not preferred, and Bruce Bell was reported for common assault after being interviewed by the police but he returned to Canada in the off season. The BIHA fined both teams for bringing the game into disrepute but none of the players were punished.

Cardiff's run of poor form carried into the play-offs.

'They were in our group in the play-offs and they just didn't have it. They beat us at home and then we went down there and it was their last game. Even if Cardiff won they weren't guaranteed to get through, we went out and scored two goals right away. Looking at our team, who had improved, and looking at their team on paper, then we shouldn't have been close. But they just didn't have the spark, I don't know what happened to them, whether they burned out or lost it mentally. I know Durham beat them at home and beat them in Cardiff, and that just didn't happen to Cardiff - they usually rebounded well. It was a surprise to everybody that they didn't make it but they didn't deserve to be there. Humberside did, they played great hockey in the play-offs, inspired hockey, Milhench came in and fired them up big time. His strength is motivation, not in coaching X's and O's and forechecks and powerplays.'

Durham topped Group A with Humberside going through to the Wembley final from second place. Durham were the first team to be sure of their place at Wembley. One of Durham's signings of the season was Kip Noble who played so well against Cardiff for the Tilburg Trappers in the European Cup last year. Kip Noble was the highest scoring defenceman for the Premier season and he scored 14 on the powerplay - a tally only bettered by Tony Hand.

In the other group Sheffield and Nottingham cruised to the semi finals. There were a record five shut-outs. Newcastle were on the wrong side twice - once against Cardiff with Welshman Stevie Lyle in goal and once against Durham with Geordie Stephen Foster between the pipes. Wayne Cowley was in goal when the Steelers shut-out Fife in Fife and then the following night at home as Steelers shut-out Nottingham. Nottingham return the favour in the Lace City the next weekend as Scott O'Connor recorded the first ever shut-out against the Steelers.

On the last weekend of the play-offs Terry Ord, who had taken over as Captain of the Warriors this season, announces his retirement from the game.

'Ordy was a great, great servant to the club. He was one of those guys who was there night in night out, wasn't overly flashy. Unless you knew a little bit about the game I don't think you could appreciate Terry Ord because he did the little things ... I have never played with a man who has broken his nose as many times as Ordy. It just seemed like every other game he was coming in the dressing room with his nose bent in another direction. He was one of those guys who if I

was a coach, he would be a coach's dream. Came to practice, worked hard, wasn't a complainer, was vocal when he had to be but didn't spout off, when he said things people usually listened to him. He put a lot of good years in for that organisation, wasn't flashy, didn't score a lot of goals, but he was always there and a solid defensive defenceman and those kind of guys are really hard to come by. He did extremely well for that club.'

The first Championship semi-final took place on the morning of Saturday 30th March between Humberside and Sheffield.

'Humberside played really well against the Steelers. It was a tight game.'

Sheffield took the first period 2-0 and the second 2-1 but the Hawks never gave up and matched Sheffield for goals in the final period to leave the scores 3-6 in Sheffield's favour.

The second semi was Saturday afternoon and saw the Durham Wasps take on the Nottingham Panthers. The game could hardly have been tighter. Paul Adey scored on the powerplay at 8 mins 13, then Seva for Durham scored again on a powerplay at 17.53. There was no further scoring until 14.21 into the third period when local Nottingham lad, Simon Hunt, put Nottingham in front and Adey sealed Durham's fate in the dying seconds of the game, getting another goal for Nottingham.

British Junior C Championship
Wembley Arena 31st March

Fife Flames...........2   Guildford Firestars 3 (1-1, 1-2, 0-0)
Guildford Scorers: Williams 1g, Johnston 1+1, Rob Lamey, 1+1, Rick Lamey 1a, Barrow 1a
Fife Scorers: Laing 1g, Gary Wishart 1g, Steven Wishart 1a
MOM: Gary Wishart FIF, Rob Lamey GUI

The Wembley final faced off on Sunday afternoon in front of 8,961 after the Junior Final had been watched by approximately 2,000 fans. Referee for the final is Simon Kirkham with Gordon Pirry and Paul Staniforth the linesmen. Steelers looked set to win the final, they were more rested than Nottingham, often cited as an unfair advantage at the Wembley weekend, and they took a commanding 3-0 lead, but the Panthers fought back at the end of the second period with an explosive three goals in 94 seconds. The teams remained tied at the end of sixty minutes and after ten minutes overtime. Penalty time.

'Shoot out, which surprised me because I don't think Sheffield should have been in that position. But that is an indication of Blazer [Nottingham Coach, Mike Blaisdell], he gets the most out of what he's got, he really does, he gets the most out of his talent. It was an excellent game, Sheffield were obviously the better team talent wise but if I remember anything about hockey in Britain when I retire, it is that the Brits always play with a great heart, regardless of the odds, they're always fighting for it and that was the case that night.'

It took nine penalty shots to divide the two teams. "King Kenny" high scoring forward for the Steelers had his shot saved as did Nottingham's leading light Paul Adey, but defencemen André Malo and Rob Wilson scored for the Steelers - Wilson's being the decider when Nottingham's 'Doc' Durdle had his attempt saved.

Referee Simon Kirkham made some kind of record, officiating in all three games. He was down to referee one semi and the final but when John Moore got hit by the puck in the second semi-final Simon laced up his skates again. Paul Staniforth also got on the ice for all three games as well. After Alan Craig received a nasty cut to his arm in the first semi and had to leave the ice for attention, Staniforth was asked to replace him. Many of the other officials were in attendance at the Wembley weekend but none had been asked to bring their skates and equipment so Simon and Paul got to officiate in every game.

With fans and players from so many clubs in attendance at the finals weekend rumours were always rife. The main one for this year, that this would be the last Wembley finals weekend, stayed a rumour for only a few months.

In the mean time both Fife and Guildford withdraw their interest from the new Superleague. The Kirkcaldy based Fife withdrew due to the limitless number of imports the new league planned to use. Guildford who had been strong supporters of the new league, dropped out when they failed to persuade the council (owners of the rink) to increase the rink capacity from 2,200. The remaining interested parties are: Sheffield, Newcastle (Durham Wasps), Cardiff, Nottingham, Basingstoke, Bracknell, Manchester and a new team based in the incomplete Ayr Centrum.

With the Superleague looming and planning permission for his arena turned down, Sir John Hall is in need of a venue for his "Durham" Wasps. In April the Warriors are "kicked out" of the Newcastle Arena.

> *'I honestly believe that Francis Smith is in the league he wants to be in right now because if he didn't want to he would have been able to stay in the Newcastle Arena. There was only one franchise right in Newcastle, and I don't think it takes a real genius to figure out that if there is a battle between Francis Smith and Sir John Hall who's going to get it. But the Wasps still needed an Arena to play in. Francis knew that joining the Superleague was joining the big time, big bucks, big salaries, big expenses, and having to run things professionally. I think he saw the beginning of what it was going to be like that season, saw that it wasn't him standing at the front door taking cash. There were a lot of things that weren't under his control and I don't think he liked that. He saw what the future of Superleague was, and that frightened him. Or it might not of frightened him, he might have been realistic, he might have said "I don't want this, I don't want to run a club at that level of professionalism." I honestly think that Francis looked at the big picture and said to himself "lets get out when I get out with some cash." The bottom line was Francis made a smart decision for himself and his sister and brother Tom. I think it was a smart business decision for him, and of course he wanted to publicly come out of it like he was hard done by, and he did, and that's great.'*

A mass meeting was held at the end of the season for those teams not involved in the Superleague. Originally there were going to be two conferences; Ahearne in the south and Wharry in the north. However the northern clubs on the whole wanted a return to low budget, limited import hockey, whilst the teams in the south wanted a wage cap of £250,000 and plenty of Europeans and dual nationals. The wrangles and debate continued for much of the summer, which added to the gloom mongers predictions that the Superleague would bring the death of British Ice Hockey. Maybe not next year, or the year after, but soon!

After a good season of ED1, the Durham *City* Wasps finish fourth in that league and lose to Wightlink Raiders in the play-off final, but in July the Durham ice rink finally closed it doors.

'Its very, very sad. Rex Brown [who took over the rink in 1994] just wanted to make it work, he just wanted to keep hockey in Durham. He lost so much of his own money. Its not just a case of hockey being gone from Durham, because it's a small, intensely proud city, really put on the map by the Wasps, people knew the Durham Wasps: it's also sad because like many small towns in Canada, the rink was the centre of social life for so many people. I know for a lot of the kids who play hockey, some go to Sunderland and some to Billingham, its really split that up. Durham was a huge developer of youth players.

The ice plant itself was held together with bubble gum and band aids, it was an ecological nightmare the amount of freon escaping into the atmosphere. It was just one thing after another after another. The people tried hard to support Durham City Wasps but its hard. I went to some games too. The whole Durham thing, so many stories, it blew my mind.'

During the summer the Newcastle United "Durham Wasps" change their name to the "Newcastle Cobras" in preparation for the move to the Newcastle Arena. There are now no ice hockey teams carrying the famous Durham team name. Bring on the Superleague, 'the King is dead, long live the King'.

1995/96

Season 1996/97

with

Steve Lyle

British Goalie for the
Cardiff Devils

	GPI	MINS	SHOTS	GA	GAA
PLAY-OFF CHAMPIONSHIP	6	360	191	15	2.50
SUPERLEAGUE	31	1833	951	85	2.78
WORLD CHAMPS POOL B	2	120	77	8	4.00

PLAY-OFF CHAMPIONSHIPS: SHEFFIELD STEELERS

SUPERLEAGUE: CARDIFF DEVILS

BENSON & HEDGES CUP: NOTTINGHAM PANTHERS

Chapter Nine

The summer of 1996 was a busy one for those involved in ice hockey. The Superleague is going to start with eight teams, with the promise of new franchises to be announced. The Superleague season will consist of the teams playing each other six times, three times home and three away, plus the Autumn Cup still sponsored by Benson & Hedges and the end of season Championship play-offs.

Beneath the Superleague, the differences between the Southern and Northern teams remained and so, confusingly, there came into being the Premier League with another eight teams (mainly from the south), and the Northern Premier League with seven teams. All three leagues introduced sudden death overtime for games drawn at the end of sixty minutes. In the Superleague this was ten minutes. An overtime winner secured two points for the win, whilst those losing still received a point; if still drawn each received one point. In the Premier League there was just five minutes sudden death, but again a winner took two points and the loser one. Unlike the Superleague, if the game was still tied penalty shots would be taken to decide a winner. In the Northern Premier League it was five minutes sudden death, but there were no penalty shots!

Stevie Lyle, started the year far away from all this brave new world in British Ice Hockey, he was at a training camp the far side of the Atlantic with the Detroit Whalers. These Whalers are a 'Major Junior League' team and a major step for someone hoping to eventually play for a team in the NHL.

> *'I went to training camp and basically I made the team but you are only allowed two Europeans per team. There was a guy who played for the farm team [a step higher] and played for them [Detroit Whalers] the year before. He was still eligible [for the Whalers] and he came back which meant that I had to move out. I think it was fate coming back. I came back to England, rejoined Cardiff and things went pretty smoothly for me. I came back and I was playing the home games and Frank Caprice was playing the away games. Then Frank had to have an operation on his knees, so I played virtually every game from there on in.'*

Whilst Stevie is in the States, Glenn Anderson, an NHL legend, was arriving on the Cardiff ice in a huge white limousine. Were the Devils really trying to sign a guy who could have bought the team without thinking about it?

> *'They were seriously trying to sign the guy and they spent a lot of money on him. He stayed for maybe three weeks but then he went to Switzerland because he was only looking for the money.'*

On 25th August 1996 the Ayr Centrum Arena was finally opened and the first game played there was on 1st September as the Ayr Scottish Eagles took on the Telford Tigers in their second game in the Benson and Hedges sponsored Autumn Cup. 2,733 people (12 short of capacity) watched as Telford from the Premier League took the first goal at 8.26, but after Eagles first goal scored by Jamie Steer at 12.44 the Eagles went on to win the game 8-2.

The Ayr team had started with a win in Newcastle the night before against a team now called the Newcastle Cobras. Ayr went on to win their first five games and going unbeaten for twelve games. The B&H Cup was divided into four groups this year, each group has two Superleague teams and two from the Premier League. All the Superleague teams come one and two in this first round. No giant killing in Ice Hockey this year. Ayr top Group A with Newcastle in second, Cardiff win all six games to top Group B with Manchester Storm in second. Sheffield Steelers beat old rivals Nottingham Panthers in to second in Group C, whilst Basingstoke also make it a clean sweep in Group D with Bracknell Bees in second. Of all the Premier teams Solihull Blaze do the best with two wins, three losses and one draw to give them five points. The management at Solihull had tried to change the name of the team to Birmingham Blaze over the summer in preparation for a planned move to the NEC and a Superleague position next season but the name change was blocked by the Solihull rink which remains their home for now.

In the two legged quarter finals of the Benson and Hedges Ayr put out Manchester, and Basingstoke beat local rivals Bracknell Bees. Nottingham beat Cardiff on penalty shots after the two games left the score line 4-4. Cardiff won the first game in Nottingham 0-1 then Nottingham won 3-4 in overtime in Cardiff. They went on to win the penalty shoot out 3-2. Sheffield have a much easier time putting out the Newcastle Cobras, winning both games.

Pool C quarter final of the European Cup is hosted by the Sheffield Steelers in October. The increase in quality in the Superleague is highlighted by the relative ease with which the Steelers won the group. In second spot were the Romanian champions Steaua Bucharest, their players were obviously talented but their equipment poor. It seemed amazing that they had even made it to the tournament looking at their ancient minibus parked next to the luxury air conditioned coach that the Tilburg Trappers arrived in from the Netherlands. During the breaks between games there were parties in the car park around Sheffield Arena with street hockey and roller hockey and the odd football game and the Romanians walked round selling hockey shirts, cigarettes and vodka. At the end of the tournament the Romanians asked to have their photo taken, not with ex-NHLer Ken Priestlay, but with the Sheffield mascot, larger than life Steeler Dan!

Back in the Superleague the powers that be decided that if a game was tied after over-time in the Play-off Championships, then, instead of going to penalties, each team would have to take one player off the ice (like in a penalty killing situation, but happening to both teams), every five minutes until there were three players and the goalie left on the ice, or a sudden death goal was scored. Unfortunately, it seems that officials of the sport had not been consulted and all the possible scenarios had not been thought through. Both GB coach Peter Woods and Nico Toeman now technical director of the BIHA openly criticised the plan. So this announcement seriously tarnished the credibility of the new Superleague organisation and the plan had evaporated by the end of the season.

'Yeah, that sounded good! That would have been fun to see. It's not really what you expect from a professional organisation. But there again they are going to

take out the redline next year (98/99). That is going to give so many breakaways, the scores are going to go way up, like it used to be.'

On the 12th October in a game between Nottingham and Cardiff, Darryl Olsen of the Panthers and Marty Yewchuk of the Devils got in to a nasty incident. Firstly Olsen used his elbow on Yewchuk as they fought for the puck along the boards, Yewchuk retaliates using his stick above shoulder height striking Olsen on the head. Yewchuk is sent to the showers but the Olsen elbow goes unpunished.

Two weeks later both players are found guilty of excessive rough play by the disciplinary committee, Yewchuk is banned for nine games and fined £1,000, whilst Olsen is fined £250.

Cardiff appealed against the finding and the appeal panel increases the punishment to some 20 ISL games. They were apparently determined to stamp out the excess of the game. But ice hockey is now big business and Cardiff, whose president is also the ISL Chairman, begin legal action against the ISL. The ISL find that they cannot uphold the ban and are forced into a climb down. One of the reasons the BIHA had agreed the move to Superleague was the increasing number of legal disputes brought into the game by the new businessmen of the sport. Now the ISL themselves know its not so easy to lay down the law!

The end of October sees Ayr put out Basingstoke in the semi-finals of the B&H Cup, but not before Basingstoke beat them 2-0 in Scotland. Ayr go on to win 9-4 in Basingstoke. Whilst Nottingham put out local rivals Sheffield, winning 3-2 away and 3-1 at home.

The beginning of November sees the Sheffield Steelers taking part in the semi-final of the European Cup. As Cardiff had done before, Sheffield found the next step a big one and came bottom of the group. However , this time the British team came away from the semis with a point, and a point taken from one of the strongest teams in Europe as they drew 2-2 with Finnish champions Hameelinna. This is the first point gained by a British team at this level of competition. The Steelers also took a 4-1 lead in their first game against Norwegian Storhamar but eventually lost the game 7-5 after the referee seemed to take exception to the physical Canadian style played by the Steelers.

A new European competition began in 1996 called the European Hockey League (EHL). Countries were selected from those appearing in World Pool A from 1994-1996 and then teams from those countries were invited to take part. For Britain it was Manchester Storm who received the invitation mainly due to the quality of the building and for setting the European indoor record attendance. The Storm took part in Group A with teams from Germany, Finland and Sweden. The games were played throughout October, November and December. Manchester played six games and lost six despite being allowed to borrow extra players from Division One especially for the European League games.

On 28th November the Manchester Storm take on the Ayr Scottish Eagles in Ayr live on Sky TV. Ayr win the first period 2-0. In the second the Storm start a come back after the Ayr goalie is penalised and Martin Smith begins the scoring for Manchester. Then one player from each side gets sent for the early shower as an altercation breaks out in front of the Ayr bench. Some five minutes later Ayr's Ryan Kummu and Manchester's Hilton Ruggles are sent to the penalty boxes for roughing. When the penalties end Kummu is quickest on to the ice and skates to the other penalty box to finish his dispute with Ruggles. The penalty box official firstly tries to shut the door on Ryan but when he fails Ryan *gets in to the box* and begins fighting with Hilton. Referee Nicholson calls the period 16 seconds early to let the tempers settle down again.

> *'Hilton is just one of these guys who winds up everyone on the ice. He is a horrible skater but a good goal scorer. I guess Hilton was mouthing and Kummu had enough. No one gets to hit Hilton - he is kind of bandy and agile and gets out the way. I guess he couldn't get out of the way in the penalty box.'*

Manchester have found the step from Division One last season to Superleague this season a harder and steeper step than anticipated and now find themselves moving in the wrong direction from third to second from the bottom of the league.

At this stage netminder Frank Caprice has played nine games for Cardiff Devils and Stevie Lyle has played just four but this is all about to change as Caprice needs an operation on his knees and Stevie steps up as number one goalie.

Steve Lyle between the pipes for Cardiff

The Benson and Hedges cup final is held on 7th December at the Sheffield Arena as the Nottingham Panthers take on the Ayr Scottish Eagles in front of 8,560 fans. Ayr are allowed to ice Ryan Kummu despite the fact that he received a six match ban for his altercation with Ruggles in the Storm game. There is some confusion between the Superleague and the Disciplinary Committee as to how and why permission was granted for Kummu to play, but the theory is that it was decided that his ban only applied to league fixtures, the first time this had ever happened.

Despite his inclusion in the team Ayr are beaten by Nottingham 5-3. Nottingham get off to a good start after Derek Laxdal puts them ahead after just 29 seconds. At 18.19 in the first period with Ayr already 3-1 down Sven Rampf was replaced in the Ayr net by Colum Cavilla because Rampf had aggravated a groin injury. The first period ended 3-1 and then the second and third both finished one a piece to leave the final score 5-3 in Nottingham's favour.

> 'That Rampf, he is one of these goalies who one game would be really hot, and the next game he could be nowhere. He was a weird goalie. He had a horrible style, like a football goalie. He'd make a save and kick the puck and it would be right down my end. If they had a different goal tender then they would have won, they were destined to win they were so good that first year.'

GB have also been playing games throughout the early stages of the season as 18 countries battle it out to secure a place in the Nagano Olympics in February 1998. On December 18th in front of 5,278 fans at the Sheffield Arena GB need a win against Switzerland to progress to the next stage of qualification. The first period ended two a piece, the second one each and in the final period Switzerland defended and defended to leave the final score 3-3 and GB failing to make it to the Olympics.

> 'We were all over them. Morrison started, Fossy [Stephen Foster] backed-up. All the players just weren't hitting the net, we were hitting the post and all sorts. When you are not playing its kind of hard to feel part of the team, but we came so close.'

Sheffield Steelers have been trying to sign a new forward, one Steve Thornton who has family in Sheffield, but his signature goes to the Cardiff Devils and Steelers sign Jason Lafreniere as they struggle to find the net with Ken Priestlay out injured. The 26th December sees Steve Thornton play against the Steelers at the Sheffield Arena for the first time and he scores all three of Cardiff's goals as Cardiff win 3-2 in overtime.

> 'That was a big weekend for us. It was just one of those games when the puck just ended up on Steve's stick and we won 3-2. Then we went to Manchester and won 2-1. I think the reason why we won the Superleague was the team character. There was no bitching or anything. Whatever happened on the ice we did as a team, we weren't the best team but we stuck together.'

The game was over shadowed by a nasty incident in the third period when Jamie Leach of the Steelers ended up with a double fracture of the cheek bone when the high stick of Cardiff's Shannon Hope made contact. Referee Andy Carson sent Hope to the showers with a five plus game, but the disciplinary committee decided that no further action was necessary which incensed Leach and his team mates. Once again the prospect of one player taking another to court for an incident during the game became a possibility. It must have been a tricky situation as Nicky Chinn still had the case brought against him by Ross Lambert hanging over him and here was his team mate considering pressing charges against another player.

At the beginning of the New Year Stevie Lyle heads off to represent GB at Under 21 level where he won tournament's best goalie at the World Junior Pool C tournament. The team had missed out on the Bronze Medal by just one goal to Denmark. First game was Belarus on December 30th who beat the GB squad 7-2. Then GB beat Austria 4-2 the next day. January 2nd and GB beat Croatia 7-0 and finally on Friday 3rd GB lose to Denmark by the narrowest of margins 5-4. Whilst the rest of the team retire to their hotel to sleep, Lyle has a long coach ride back to the Romanian capital to catch a plane back to the UK, so he can make it back to Cardiff in time to turn out for the Devils 7pm Saturday night against the Ayr Scottish Eagles.

> 'I had to travel home with all the referees! I was really tired and Paul [Heavey] kept asking me "Are you sure you're OK?" I let in an awful goal in that game. They took a shot from outside the blue line and it took a funny bounce and … oh embarrassment right there.'

The Superleague announce in January that another Ice Hockey franchise has been sold. Leeds United football team have plans for their Elland Road ground that include an indoor arena suitable for ice hockey. Planning permission is not currently granted for the development but Leeds plan to have their new team up and running in time for the 1998/99 season.

On January 18th Cardiff are back at the Sheffield Arena and it quickly turns into a very different game from the tight 3-2 December 26th game. The Steelers take the first period six goals to one. However the second period goes to the Devils 2-1 and they keep the Steelers off the score sheet in the third period 3-0 to lose the game 7-6.

> 'It brought us back down to earth. It was an experience! I thought for sure I was going to get pulled. I tried to keep focused and its hard in Sheffield because of the fans. I'm glad I stayed in that game, and at the end, even though Sheffield won, it felt like we won because we got back together as a team and fought back, I think another two minutes and we would have brought it back and it would have gone into overtime. You've got to take the highs and the lows, but not usually in the same game!'

At the beginning of February, Cardiff shut out the Ayr Scottish Eagles at home 4-0. With Stevie between the pipes in the Cardiff net, this gave him his second shut-out of the season. The only other netminder with two Superleague shut-outs to his name was Stephen Foster of Newcastle, the only other British trained goalie getting regular ice time with a Superleague team.

> 'Yeah that was funny with all these big Canadian goalies coming over. Me and Fossy were playing for ourselves, to show people that British players can do it. Frank [Caprice] played Basingstoke away and got a shut-out then the next night I played Bracknell at home and shut them out 8-0. Then Ayr made it two for me.'

By the end of the month Cardiff have wrapped up the first Superleague title and taken it home. They win the league at home against Manchester Storm on February 20th taking the game 6-4.

'It didn't matter who we won against. It would have been nice to have been Sheffield because they enjoy celebrating in front of us and rubbing it in our faces! It was weird because I've never won anything so big, and all of a sudden, being the goalie, the entire team is jumping on top of you and all you can think is "I can't breathe"!'

Superleague	GP	W	L	D	OTL	GF	GA	Pts
Cardiff Devils	42	30	9	3	1	208	130	64
Sheffield Steelers	42	27	11	4	2	168	127	60
Ayr Scottish Eagles	42	21	15	6	0	171	157	48
Nottingham Panthers	42	21	20	1	2	160	147	45
Newcastle Cobras	42	17	23	2	5	158	172	41
Bracknell Bees	42	15	25	2	1	169	202	33
Manchester Storm	42	14	25	3	1	142	191	32
Basingstoke Bison	42	11	28	3	3	152	202	28

Note: If scores tied at the end of overtime each team received one point for the draw. A winner in overtime gets two points (W) and the loser one point (OTL).

Steve Lyle celebrates Cardiff's Superleague win with fans

Top of the goaltending averages for the season is one Stevie Lyle of Cardiff. Top of the scoring chart for the league is Dale Junkin of the Bracknell Bees with 27 goals, 33 assists for a total of 60 points, whilst Tony Hand who had been top for the last four years is knocked out of the top ten with just 45 points. Cardiff had three players in the top five with second placed Vezio Sacratini chalking up 58 points, Ivan Matulik in fourth and Doug McCarthy in fifth both with 54 points, Ivan having played one less game.

In the British Ice Hockey writers association awards Jim Lynch wins the Superleague coach of the year award.

'He has done amazing since he has been in Ayr. He seems a good coach, what I've seen, on the bench he gives them a lot of confidence and he has picked some good guys.'

The Alan Weeks Trophy for Best British Defenceman went to Cardiff's Jason Stone.

'He knows he needs to be a bit faster with his feet, but he has a good defensive head on him, he is not like your Kip Noble who gets the puck and is off up the other end, he always stays back. This year [97/98], he's been telling me, he hasn't seen so much of the ice. He is one of these guys who needs confidence to play well and when he is confident he is one of the best defencemen in the league.'

In the Premier League Swindon IceLords were running away with the title. They iced an almost entirely Canadian team and were backed by computer games firm EA Sports. Solihull Blaze were up there with Swindon in the first half of the season but they ran out of steam - and eventually money - as the planned move to the Birmingham NEC fell through. The players finished the season with little pay coming through to them and then they pulled out of the play-offs. The Swindon IceLords made it through the play-offs unlike Solihull but then they too went to the wall as backer Bob Dewar pulled out.

In the Northern Premier League the Fife Flyers with a long history of developing talent were strongly placed to take the league which limited each team to three overseas players. Fife also benefited from having Martin McKay, who played last season for British Champions Sheffield Steelers, as number one netminder. Crowds in Fife regularly topped 2,000 whilst Blackburn Hawks, who came second to Manchester Storm in Division One last year, managed only 800 per game in a 3,000 seater rink. The Hawks claimed they still worked within budget as they signed Scandinavian imports rather than the more typical and expensive Canadians.

With only eight teams in the Superleague all teams qualify for the Play-offs. In Group A are new team Ayr, Manchester Storm, Newcastle and Cardiff Devils. Group B consists of local rivals Basingstoke and Bracknell, together with local rivals Nottingham and Sheffield. Cardiff take Group A with Ayr Scottish Eagles in second after fighting it out with Newcastle for the second spot. After the disappointment of losing the second semi-final against Nottingham in Wembley last year, for the Cobras failure to make it to the semi-finals this year was a disaster for the high spending Newcastle team. In Group B it could be said to be 'business as usual' as the two great rivals once again make it through to the Play-off semi-finals with Nottingham just pipping Sheffield for top of the table honours.

The Superleague Play-off semi-finals are to take place at the Manchester Arena on March 22nd and then the final is to take place, again in Manchester, but a week later on the 29th March.

The first semi-final sees the Cardiff Devils take on the Sheffield Steelers. During the season the Devils had taken four out of six games between the two teams but there had never been more than a goal between the two teams. The first period is scoreless with both teams creating their chances, but the penalty count is high from referee Graham Horner. The Steelers are the first to break the deadlock after two minutes of the second period, and go on to take the second period 3-1. Despite increasing pressure from Cardiff in the third period Steelers, with the form they had shown in the European competition early in the season, defend and extend their lead taking the third 2-1 and the game 5-2.

> 'We didn't play very well and, not saying it just because we lost, but the refereeing was just horrible that night, he had a bad game. We couldn't get a strategy going and everyone was just 'agghhh' and we didn't know what to do or where to look.'

The second semi-final faced off directly after the first between Nottingham Panthers and the Ayr Scottish Eagles. The Eagles out shot the Panthers 20-8 in the first period but came away with only the one goal as Trevor Robins performed miracles in the Nottingham net. In the second period Nottingham picked up their game but found Rampf in the net for Ayr was also on form and the period ended 3-2 to Ayr. Ayr scored first in the third period and Nottingham's fate seemed settled, but Nottingham coach Mike Blaisdell called for a stick measure on Ryan Kummu and, for the second time in as many weeks, his stick was found to be illegal. Mike Bishop began the fight back in the 56th minute and 41 seconds later Neil Morgan reduced the deficit to one goal. Then with little more than two minutes left on the clock the game was tied by Mike Bishop.

The Superleague had decided, just two days before, that there would be no penalty shoot-outs and each game would be played to a conclusion. This created great excitement at the Nynex as the two teams lined up for sudden death overtime, part one. There was no score in the first ten minute period of overtime, nor in the second, nor the third, nor fourth … Many neutral fans drifted away from the Nynex before public transport shut down for the night, or as their buses had to return home, whilst those who remained were determined to see it through, to be able to say "I was there, I saw it all". No penalties had been called as the teams played 'safe' hockey, but eventually referee Andy Carson decided Mike Bishops challenge on Sam Groleau had to be called and Ayr had a power play in the sixth period of overtime. However after Garth Premak dove to the ice to block a slapshot from Jiri Lala, Dallman set up Jeff Hoad for a short-handed break away. His first shot was saved by Rampf but the rebound returned to the Nottingham forward, and he finished the game at 115.49 . As the Nottingham team celebrated both Mike Bishop and Mike Blaisdell charged towards referee Carson to protest at the penalty call. Not wanting to get into a heated debate that may lead to Blaisdell or Bishop getting a misconduct penalty that might see them penalised in the final next week the referee did his best to skate away from both. Maybe he shouldn't have worried. Despite several players openly criticising the refereeing of the semi-finals, they received no punishment from the Superleague, because their rules did not cover this situation! Sky had televised both semi-finals and continued coverage through all the overtime which took the coverage until 11.15pm.

'I watched it. I thought Ayr were going to win. If Ayr had won the semi, they would have won the final. I wanted Ayr to win it, because Ayr that year were Sheffield's bogey team, whereas Nottingham don't have a good record against Sheffield. As soon as Nottingham won I knew it would be Sheffield winners in the final.'

Prior to the Superleague final there was the junior final and then the two Premier league winners Fife Flyers and Swindon IceLords played to decide the overall Premier Champions. The Sunderland Arrows had had an excellent season with ex Durham Mosquitoes coach Roly Barrass at the helm. They won all fourteen games in the northern conference and only dropped their first point of the season in the away game of the English final as they drew with Guildford 6-6, they then went on to win at home 4-2 to make it to the British final against the Fife Flames. Arrows Michael Bowman scored at least one goal in every game.

British Junior C Championship
Wembley Arena 31ˢᵗ March

Fife Flames……..2   Guildford Firestars…….3 (1-1, 1-2, 0-0)
Guildford Scorers: Williams 1g, Johnston 1+1, Rob Lamey 1+1, Rick Lamey 1a, Barrow 1a
Fife Scorers: Laing 1g, Gary Wishart 1g, Steven Wishart 1a
MOM: Gary Wishart FIF, Rob Lamey GUI

In front of 5,438 fans, the Premier final merely goes to demonstrate the difference between the two leagues. Although Fife come out playing hard, the IceLords just grind them down and eventually win the game 5-0. Ice Hockey players who have not reached the age of 21 are required to play with full facemasks. Fife, who have such a good record in junior finals, had several young players in full facemasks playing for the team, and despite 29 year old Martin McKay in goal and Derek King (26) in defence, the average age of the Fife team was closer to 21. Swindon on the other hand relied on their ten strong Canadian contingent although Brit Robin Davison scored the first and Brit Lee Braithwaite made it onto the score sheet for Swindon with the fifth and final goal of the game. This was the last game of professional ice hockey for Martin McKay before joining the police force and the Fife fans were joined by those Sheffield fans who had arrived early for the Superleague final, to give him a warm send off. At the end of the game referee Mike Rowe is awarded the Mick Curry Memorial Trophy for the most improved official. Does the name ring a bell? Back in Chapter One the very same Mike Rowe is coming second in the penalty minutes table as a player for Whitley Bay, one of those 'poacher turned game keeper' moments!

For the Superleague final the crowd had swelled to 14,116, many more than could be accommodated in the old Wembley Arena, which must have been a relief to Superleague who had been strongly criticised by many ice hockey fans and pundits for the move. Referee for the final was Simon Kirkham with linesmen Dave Stevenson and Paul Staniforth.

As the game began it seemed as if the Sheffield team agreed with Stevie Lyle that with Nottingham as opposition the Championship was already theirs. This despite Derek Laxdal putting Nottingham on the score board first after just 56 seconds. Sheffield tied the period through a Ron Shudra goal at 15.57 and the teams went in to the first break tied at one. The second period saw Kovacs and Lafreniere add to the Steeler's tally and with a goalless third period the Steelers had the Championship won 3-1.

During the finals weekend an on ice presentation was made to Storm coach John Lawless as the British Ice Hockey Writers have inducted him into their Hall of Fame. John came to Britain in 1982 playing for the Peterborough Pirates. After three seasons at Peterborough he moved with Dennis Adams to the new Wales National Ice Rink and masterminded the birth of the Cardiff Devils. After huge success with the Devils he then moved to the Nynex in Manchester and led them to the Division One title in their first year. Certainly an impressive resume but in hockey you are only as good as your last season and the Storm had struggled in their first year of Superleague. Shortly after this presentation is made he is sacked by the Storm and returns to Canada to work with his brother's firm.

From April 12th -21st the GB squad competed in the World Championship Pool B hosted by Katowice and Sosnowiec in Poland. First up were the host nation and the lively crowd helped Poland take a 4-3 win on the opening day of the tournament. The next day GB take on Kazakhstan and go down 4-2, man of the match for GB was netminder Stevie Lyle.

The 15th April at Sosnowiec and Great Britain obtain their first points with an 8-2 win over the Netherlands with Patrick Scott scoring a hat-trick and both Bill Morrison and Stephen Foster gaining ice time in the GB net. Morrison was again on netminding duties the next day as GB take on and beat Denmark 9-1.

On April 18th it was goalie Stephen Foster who gains the man of the match for GB as they draw 2-2 with Austria in a very tight game. It must have been a disappointing result for the team though as they had been leading 2-0 mid way through the second period.

Next up were the Swiss and after the disappointment of being put out of the Olympic qualifying by them earlier in the season, the GB team were fired up for this game. However it was the Swiss who came away with the points winning 3-2. If the Great Britain team were to make it in to the qualification group for Pool A then they were going to have to beat top of the table Belarus. Unfortunately this was not to be after the opposition chalked up four goals in a six minute spell. Belarus win 6-2, and Britain finish third from the bottom of Pool B.

1996/97

Player of the year, despite his late start to the season, is seventeen year old Stevie Lyle of the Superleague Champions Cardiff Devils.

'I was very surprised and I never even thought about it before I got it. The nicest thing about it, we get all these Canadians coming and it stayed with the British, and it was good because I was the first goalie to get it. Apparently, I won by two votes over Trevor Robins, the Nottingham goalie, I would have thought he'd get it over me, but I suppose I got it because we won the first Superleague.'

Stevie Lyle is a prime example of what the young British players can achieve, given their chance. How did he get started and progress to be the first goalie to win the player of the year of the award for the first year of the new Superleague.

'I put on a pair of cricket pads and players gloves and went in goal. If I had got hurt then, I would never have gone back in but I didn't, and here I am. My parents never had a holiday for eight years because there is so much goalie equipment and you are always growing out of it. They didn't want me to wear stuff if it was getting small because that's when you get injured. Jeff Smith was my idol, and he used to come on the ice with me sometimes and tell me "If I wanted it, I had to work for it."

All the senior players came down and helped a bit - Hilton Ruggles, Nicky Chinn, Steve Moria, Doug McEwen, even Shannon Hope (when I was really young) and that was surprising because he is just everywhere! It was good because kids listen to the players a little more because they're you're idol. Its funny because Shannon has been there since day one for me, and I used to watch him talk to the goalie before a game, and I always wanted for him to do that for me. Now I actually play with him I know he doesn't say much, talks rubbish, but it looks good!

It was nice to win the Superleague and know that you have helped the team to do it. I played for three years and didn't win a thing. The first year we went to Wembley, and I've always wanted to play in Wembley, but lost to the penalty shoot out, Jason Wood was in goal. We lost in the semi-finals. And then we didn't even make it to Wembley. Durham, playing out of Sunderland, made it. Then there was no more Wembley.

The league is getting better, but the budget just doesn't balance and its hard on the British players, because I don't know, British players are just another player now. Look at Tony Hand now, he's just another player. When I played against him playing for Murrayfield, I didn't care about anyone else shooting on me - just shut-out Tony Hand.

Give British players a chance. The Canadians set the standard and you learn so much from them and you can't do anything but learn from them, but they should still be giving the Brits a chance. Like I got my chance with John Lawless. We were practising going into the European Cup and we were practising the penalty shoot out. He had scored against me and there was Ian Cooper left and he [John Lawless] said if you save this I'll give you the start in Europe. Coops comes down and I stopped it. I hope I'm not, but I could be the last Cardiff kid coming through.'

Season 1997/98
with
Scott Young
Canadian Defenceman for the
Ayr Scottish Eagles

	GP	G	A	Pts	PIM
Play-Off Championship	9	3	6	9	8
Superleague	28	7	16	23	77
Express Cup	17	6	6	12	52
Benson & Hedges Cup	15	2	6	8	43
Totals	69	18	34	52	180

PLAY-OFF CHAMPIONSHIPS: Ayr Scottish Eagles

SUPERLEAGUE: Ayr Scottish Eagles

EXPRESS CUP: Ayr Scottish Eagles

BENSON & HEDGES CUP: Ayr Scottish Eagles

Chapter Ten

During the summer there had been much uproar when the Sheffield Steelers were granted a place in the European League (the European Cup having been scrapped) as Play-off Champions instead of Cardiff Devils the League Champions. Sheffield decline their invitation and Cardiff are offered the place if they agree to play their home games at Manchester's Nynex Arena. This generates much public outcry about venues rather than teams gaining entry to European competition, particularly as Manchester have again been given a wild card entry into the European competition despite their poor performance the previous year. Somehow communication between international organisations, the Superleague, the BIHA and the Cardiff club breaks down and Manchester become our only representatives in the European League for the 97/98 season.

Below the Superleague, the BIHA have been working hard to bring the Northern and Southern Premier League teams back together. This year they are to play in regional groups, playing each team in their own group twice and each team in the other group once.

The 97/98 season was the second for Ayr Scottish Eagles. Coach Jim Lynch signed nine new players, including Jeff Hoad from Nottingham who had scored the goal that put Ayr out in the semi-finals of the Championship in Manchester in the sixth period of overtime. Four new players were new faces to British Ice Hockey, including new goalie Rob Dopson. The thirty year old came from Houston Aeros in the IHL; his CV includes spells in the East Coast Hockey League and briefly in the NHL when he turned out twice for the Pittsburgh Penguins in 1993.

Scott Young had joined the Ayr Scottish Eagles in their first year and looking at the team sheet for the new year he thought the team would do well.

> 'I didn't think we'd be doing what we are doing. I knew we'd be a good team. I knew we would be in the top four, for sure, we've got a good line up from the goalie forward, a solid line up and a lot of depth and even if we had injuries we had no weaknesses, and we've had guys injured all year. All the other teams seem to be belly aching about injuries, well we've had injuries all year too - we've just played through them. I thought maybe we'd have a chance to win something but not it all.'

The Centrum Arena, built between Ayr and Prestwick, home to the Ayr Scottish Eagles, has more history as a building than the Devils and Steelers do as teams. Ayr originally played out of a magnificent 5,000 seater stadium at Beresford Terrace, but that closed down in 1972, the Ayr team continued as best they could in the new smaller Limekiln Road. In 1988/89 the Ayr Bruins were playing out of the small Limekiln Road rink with a spectator capacity of 700 and an ice pad 49 metres by 26: the team were anticipating moving into the new arena during the next season. For the 1989/90 season Ayr Bruins became the Ayr Raiders in anticipation of the move to the new Centrum Arena. However, on the 6th November 1990 Glen Henderson, the businessman behind the new arena, found his bank putting his business into receivership and the half built

Centrum Arena up for sale. The Raiders played on through 91/92 playing home games in Glasgow with a 1,000 capacity and 56 x 26 metre ice pad. For 1992/93 they found a new home at the new Paisley Rink which is similar in size to the Glasgow rink with Jack Dryburgh as coach and three quality imports including Chris Norton. David Gardner-Brown was to be their saviour and see them safely into the 'promised land' of the Centrum Arena, but the Raiders ran out of money and in November of that season the BIHA expelled them from the league and the team dispersed. In 1993 the Centrum Arena was purchased by the Barr Construction group and work began to complete the half built arena with a £500,000 grant from the National Lottery. Ayr applied to join the new Superleague and with the backing of William Barr OBE the Ayr Scottish Eagles were born.

At the beginning of the 97/98 season, looking at the line-ups, who did Scott Young think would be making the grade?

'The usual teams; Cardiff, Sheffield, Nottingham, but Sheffield's having a pretty bad year and Cardiff was always good for a point but just lately they have been beaten by Bracknell again. It just shows you the parity in the league right now, even ... like, Newcastle they've been the worst team all year, but when you play them they don't seem that bad, they just seem to lose. Its not like its a cake walk every time you play them. Its not like the old days when you just knew, you just knew, its not like that at all any more. You've got to play every night or you've got no chance of winning.'

Nottingham Panthers hit financial troubles over the summer and at one stage were apparently telling their imports not to fly into the country as using the tickets would tip the club financially over the edge. After a couple of weeks of abortive attempts, the club's future was secured by Aladdin Sports Management.

In season 96/97 each Superleague team had played the others three times home and away. Add the B&H Cup games, the Play-off games and the fans began to lose interest in local derbies and rivalries that in previous years would have been real crowd pullers. It was decided therefore to play each team home and away twice as had been the case in the old Premier Division. There was a gap in the published schedule around December, the Superleague planned to fill it with an international competition with French and Dutch teams as a replacement for the third home and away fixtures. The Dutch pulled out almost immediately, and then nothing further was heard as to what was to happen.

'I don't think those other teams had the money. I know the Dutch teams don't have much money but I don't know about the French. I don't know why they bailed out but I'm assuming that's why.'

For the new season the Superleague also brings in a new system of fines for certain offences on the ice. Whoever is fined has to pay the fine with a cheque from their own account in an attempt to stop the teams paying players fines on their behalf.

'Its OK to have fines, that's great, fines and bans for serious incidents, but they've got fines for guys getting hit from behind, nowhere near the boards or the net.

134

Yeah, I got fined twice this year! I can see that if the guys going head first in the boards and you smash him head first into the boards, but a two minute cross-check !?! There should be fines for serious incidents like high sticking - if you cut the guy and he bleeds, you should be fined for that because you shouldn't be cutting guys but all this other stuff ... They've got to get that sorted out for next year because that's all wrong. Can you imagine being fined for doing the job they pay you to do?'

The season started as usual with the first rounds of the Benson and Hedges sponsored Autumn Cup. The Superleague teams were divided into two groups with two Premier teams in each group. In Group A Telford Tigers and Paisley Pirates manage two points each at the bottom of the group. Top of the group Manchester Storm start the season well, with Ayr and Newcastle having the same points below them. In Group B Cardiff finish on the same points as Nottingham (14) and Slough do the best of all the Premier teams with four points, whilst Peterborough only manage to chalk up one point for a draw at home.

'Its like the FA Cup, its a chance for the little teams to play the big teams. Because its a different game, a good hockey team will never, ever be beaten by a bad hockey team. In soccer games one or two goals is the norm so the team in the lower division can score a goal and just shut them out. In the course of a season they'd do terrible in the [football] Premiership, but on any given night they might just sneak it. In hockey they can't shut you out, its impossible, unless their goalie completely stands on his head or something. Its just the way it is.'

After four games of the regular season Ayr go top of the league. They are quickly overtaken by Manchester, an early sign of which teams would be there or thereabouts come the season end.

'I'm a firm believer in a good start, winning is contagious: you find ways to win, when you are losing you find ways to lose. Points at the beginning of the season are huge, I don't care what anybody says. If you get behind the eight ball off the hopper, you better get going in a hurry. You get excited about being in first place. You don't want to lose at the beginning of the season. Look at Manchester - they started off hot, they went into a little bit of a slide, not a huge slide, but they tailed off for a while. Now they've picked it up and finished up second. When they went to slide they already had points in their pocket, so teams have to catch up and then they [Manchester] pick it up again and pull away. But if you are losing and you go on a roll then you are just catching up with those other teams and that is so much harder.'

October sees the trial of Nicky Chinn over the Ross Lambert incident finally come to court (see chapter 8). The players continue to play at the weekends whilst spending the week in a Leeds Courtroom. On the day of the verdict the whole Sheffield Steelers team turn up to support Nicky who was found not guilty. Scott Young thinks it should never have come to court.

'If you get stuck in the face, it should not happen, but you can't be bringing the law in to it. Yeah maybe he should have been fined and banned for a while but

you don't take it to court. Since you were a kid you knew it might happen one day, and I'm just a believer of not bringing the law into it.'

Manchester Storm are in Group F of the European League with HC Sparta Prague of the Czech Republic, HC Bolzano of Italy and Dynamo Moscow of Russia. In their first game they took a point for an overtime loss in Bolzano, their second game is an overtime loss to Dynamo Moscow in the Storm Shelter and then after going so close in the first two games, finally, a win against HC Sparta Prague in Prague on October 28th.

In the quarter finals of the B&H Cup Ayr beat Nottingham home and away. Bees played the Storm at home first and that game finished 2-2 after the game was interrupted several times by power cuts, Manchester Storm went through after beating the Bees 5-4 at the Storm Shelter. There was a draw between Newcastle and Basingstoke 1-1 but Newcastle Cobras won away from home 1-5 to go through. Cardiff put out old rivals Sheffield, winning both at home and away.

In the semi finals of the B&H Cup Manchester play Ayr at home ending in a 4 all draw. The second leg is live on Sky, from the Centrum Arena and after the end of the first period a build-up of cigarette smoke in the bar sets off the fire alarms. Only Sky presenter, Gabby Yorath (and the camera man?) are in the building as the adverts end and Sky go back live to Ayr!!! The interval is extended by five minutes after the firemen give the all clear and everyone returns to their seats. Ayr go on to win 4-2. In the other semi-final Cardiff take a 6-2 lead to Newcastle and the Cobras can only manage a 3-2 win.

Cobras poor run of form in the league sees Rick Brebant sacked in November.

'I don't hear anything good about Rick Brebant as a guy. Don't get me wrong, he is a good hockey player, but guys don't want to play for him, but losing is a disease like winning is contagious. You don't have to be a master coach to coach here. It is all about recruiting the right players, with the right attitude. A team that is good and gets along is very, very important. You don't have to be a master coach to have a winning team, you have to get the guys to want to play for you.'

The Express Cup begins in November as a replacement for the international event planned by the Superleague. Unfortunately the first round involves each Superleague team playing the others home and away once. This is of course the third home and away fixture the Superleague had been trying to avoid, and made worse by the fact that tickets went on sale just before Christmas, the most financially draining time of the year for many fans.

'Who gives a cup! That's what it started out like but I think once it got going teams want to win it, its a trophy. I want to win anything I'm in, it doesn't matter what it is. If I played chequers with my girlfriend I'd want to win. Most athletes are like that, you have to want to win, or there is nothing to drive you to get in your gear everyday and practice for two hours.'

'I think if they'd have said there was going to be an Express Cup earlier I think it would have been bigger in the beginning than it was. Its gained momentum as its

gone along, teams were trying really hard to get into the semi-final. I think its because it was a last minute thing. If they have it next year it will be better.'

The end of November saw Ayr topping the Express Cup table and struggling Newcastle at the bottom. However Ayr had already played five games in the cup whilst Newcastle had only played one! Coach of the Ayr Scottish Eagles made the Express Cup the "back-up netminders competition" with Colum Cavilla between the pipes for all of Ayr's Express Cup games.

The fans in Sheffield did not take to the early rounds of the cup, 3,777 on Wednesday 10th and 3,851 on Saturday 13th whilst in the Superleague on Sunday 14th 8,280 are at the House of Steel to see Sheffield take on the Nottingham Panthers. The Steelers inconsistent performances took a nose dive as the Panthers seemed to run riot. Frustration and bad temper began to take over and at 44.05 there was a bench clearance of both teams.

'I've never been coached by Clyde [Tuyl] or [Alex] Dampier, I don't know what they're like. They've got a decent team but not a great team. I just think Damps focused too much on having a tough team rather than a good team. We don't have one tough guy on our team and we are in first place, Manchester doesn't have one guy and they are in second place. We've got a bunch of fiesty guys but we don't have one guy whose sole purpose is to be tough. You might need one guy but you don't want a team full because they can't play. If you can get real tough guys that can play then you are laughing, but most of them are not available because they're playing in the NHL.'

December 6th sees the final of the B&H Cup at the Sheffield Arena as Ayr take on Cardiff in front of 6,193 fans. The game began with both teams playing defensively.

'Nobody wants to make the mistake. It was the first trophy up for grabs. You want to win so bad you don't want to make the mistake to lose. Guys were playing safe and making sure they played safe and that's why there weren't goals.'

The goals finally began at 31.20 as Cardiff's Doug McEwen put the first marker on the board. The game picked up pace with Ayr throwing everything they could at Cardiff. At 48.03 Shannon Hope of Cardiff gets a 5 + game penalty for high sticks right in front of referee Simon Kirkham and the live Sky TV audience! Parco equalises for Ayr at 51.27 Then at 57.18 Hoad scores the winner for Ayr. Villain of the previous season becomes hero of this for the Ayr fans.

On December 9th Manchester Storm play their last game in the European League. They have lost only one game in regular time but the overtime losses and three wins are not enough to see them progress to the next round as Dynamo Moscow win the Division with four straight wins and two wins in overtime.

By the end of January the Express Cup table still has Ayr on top, played 10 games and 9 wins. Nottingham and Sheffield have both played 12 with 7 wins and 5 losses, whilst Cobras are still propping up the table having played 9 and won none, recording 8

1997/98

losses and a draw. Ayr have now taken poll position at the top of the Superleague table as well. This is despite having Dennis Purdie, David St Pierre, Matt Hoffman, Hoad and Bauba all missing games for Ayr in January. So how come Ayr just rolled on through the injuries?

'One thing maybe because none of our defencemen got hurt, except Kummu for a couple of games, and our goalie hasn't been hurt, so the heart of our defence that keeps us in games - nobody was hurt. All of our forwards could play on any other team so, when you put someone else out there, there is no weakness. We may not have the numbers but we are not weak, we're not weak in any position.'

In one week at the Storm Shelter the Manchester Storm shut-out three different teams, with Jim Hrivnak between the pipes in all three games. Firstly on January 20th they win 2-0 against Newcastle, then in 22nd Hrivnak saves 47 shots on goal for the Storm to beat Bracknell 5-0, finally on the 25th the shut-out continues against the Steelers as Storm take it 4-0.

On February 8th Manchester play at Ayr. If Ayr win this one they clinch their second trophy of the season to take the league title. However, this time with Grant Sjerven as netminder Manchester spoil the party by taking the game 2-1. The league title is taken by Ayr on 15th against Newcastle Cobras, despite an impressive defensive performance from the Cobras who prevented Ayr from scoring until 42.19. Ayr scored the second when Newcastle pulled their net minder and Dennis Purdie scored with just three seconds left on the clock.

Superleague Player of the Year - Ayr Goalie, Rob Dopson

Superleague	GP	W	L	D	OTL	GF	GA	Pts
Ayr Scottish Eagles	28	20	7	1	2	117	69	43
Manchester Storm	28	18	7	3	1	123	80	40
Cardiff Devils	28	15	11	2	2	99	79	34
Nottingham Panthers	28	14	11	3	0	95	99	31
Bracknell Bees	28	14	13	1	1	95	115	30
Sheffield Steelers	28	11	15	2	3	103	101	27
Basingstoke Bison	28	5	19	4	6	80	116	20
Newcastle Cobras	28	6	20	2	1	66	119	15

Note: If scores tied at the end of overtime each team received one point for the draw. A winner in overtime gets two points (W) and the loser one point (OTL).

Tony Hand returns to the top of the leading scorers chart with fewer points than he scored last year, just nine goals, 30 assists to give 39 points in 28 games. In second place is team mate Ed Courtenay who clocked up 23 goals, 14 assists for 37 points in just 24 games.

February also saw Anschutz Sports who run the LA Kings in the NHL announcing their plans to run a Superleague hockey team from the London Arena in the Docklands, starting next season 98/99. The Docklands Arena was not built with permanent ice facilities and so a major refurbishment of the venue begins in preparation for the new venture.

After the first home and away round of the Express Cup the top four teams go into semi finals played over two legs home and away. Top of the table Ayr take on fourth placed Nottingham. Ayr go through after a 4-4 first leg in Nottingham and a 12-4 win in the second leg. Nottingham are suffering with injuries, including their number one goalie Trevor Robins. Back-up goalie British born and trained Scott O'Connor could not prevent the mighty Ayr from reaching the Express Cup final. Nottingham had also signed former Ayr junior, Peter Russell from Glasgow as temporary back-up netminder and he replaced O'Connor with just over twelve minutes left in the second leg with the score 9-3 to Ayr.

The second semi final saw Sheffield Steelers go 3-1 down in Bracknell setting up an exciting second leg in the House of Steel. But the Steelers just can't make home ice count finishing the first period 2-2 the second and third 1-1 and Bracknell Bees go through to their first final.

Having put in a record breaking performance for the Storm, Jim Hrivnak is then sacked by the Manchester Storm on Saturday 21st February. Hrivnak became the fourth player to leave the Storm following Brad Turner, Rick Judson and Dominic Maltais. Coach Kurt Kleinendorst said at the time, "The only negative thing is that I don't like the reflection that this is the fourth player to leave. I don't think in my coaching career I've had four players leave let alone four players in one season but at the end of the day you've got to think of the success of the team."

1997/98

Scott Young seems to echo the winning sentiments:

'They were playing good and winning and that's the bottom line, it doesn't really matter if some guys aren't happy. They haven't won anything, but they've beat us a couple of times and they've done well in Europe. Its hard to keep twenty guys happy, its really hard to keep twenty guys happy.'

Despite the fact that deadline day for signing is long past, Storm sign a back-up netminder John Lorenzo. As an EU passport holder he did not require a work permit, but is unlikely to appear on the ice much as he was signed under the Superleague Rule 6.9 covering temporary transfers and will only play if Grant Sjerven has an illness or injury backed up by a doctors certificate.

On February 26th the Express Cup Final between Ayr Scottish Eagles and the Bracknell Bees takes place at the Newcastle Arena .

'We were confident in our ability, confident but not cocky. We were worried about Bracknell as they were on a roll, we didn't even take Newcastle [in the play-offs] lightly. We work hard, we've got good players, but none of us are great or we wouldn't probably be here. We know you've got to work hard to win, none of the teams are bad.'

Joey Mittelsteadt put Ayr into the lead after only 32 seconds. Ayr then went on to lead 3-0 with the Bracknell players still slightly shell shocked to be in their first final and down one goal so quickly. However, the Bracknell fight back began some ten minutes into the second period when they put Ayr goalie Cavilla under pressure. Then Joe Ferraccioli put the first past Cavilla at 33.04. Burke scored Bracknell's second just before the break, which led to a storming third period with Bees swarming all over Ayr as Ayr had over Cardiff in the B&H final. The Bees were unable to grab victory from the all conquering Ayr and the final period remained scoreless despite Bracknell pulling their net minder and having two quality shots on goal in the last fifteen seconds.

The low turn out for the Express Cup, together with on going negotiations with the Arena over costs and an unhappy owner, mean that the Steelers are up for sale. George Dodds, one of the main founders of the Superleague feels he can no longer spend his families money on the Steelers and looks for partners, but none seem forthcoming.

February 28th sees the Superleague play-offs begin and the second bench clearance of the season, the first for Newcastle but the Steelers and referee Mike Rowe had been there once before this season. The next night Newcastle found themselves in trouble again when a disciplined performance disintegrated in the last ten minutes at Ayr. At the final hooter the Cobras left the ice without shaking hands and both Chris Norton and Rob Trumbley got misconduct penalties for verbally abusing the officials.

Throughout the year there had been a series of strange goings on; one player was disciplined for biting an official, players kicking each other (a major offence due to the razor sharp blades attached to a hockey players feet), one player received a ban for cross checking an official, and two players were disciplined for punching officials.

Scott Young in action for Ayr

'There is no excuse for doing those things to officials, don't get me wrong, but I don't think they understand that hockey is an emotional game. You're fired up and some guy trips you or something when you had a chance to score, and they don't call it. What do they think, that you are not going to get up and get angry. The guy will have mugged you, tripped you and stopped you from scoring, you'll get up and mouth off and they'll give you a penalty.

If they would be on the same level as us and understand you might have an outburst once in a while. You don't give us ten minutes straight away, you say "shut-up or I'll give you ten minutes", then you shut-up or take your ten minutes. I'd say the officiating is better than it used to be, at times they are not bad, but other times you are going "do they even know anything about the game?" I know its a hard job and I know nobody's perfect ... they've got to put some money into it and improve a bit.'

But the aggravation is not limited to the ice. One of the Ayr staff was run over loading the bus in Nottingham.

'He was just loading a bag on the bus, and a Nottingham fan ran him over, there are weird people in the world. Most of the crowd [at Nottingham] are really nice but there are a few people near the bench at Nottingham that mouth us off every time we leave the ice and stuff. I just about battered one the other day, but that is what he's trying to do, egg me on and then he'll take me to court. So I let it go, but I got the steward to tell him, to get him to get out, or he was going to get a stick in the mouth.'

In Group A of the Superleague Play-offs Ayr and Sheffield take the top two slots, but Nottingham, with Robins back in goal, and Newcastle, push hard. In Group B Cardiff and Manchester have an easier time of it against Basingstoke and Bracknell. Basingstoke, who had also signed a foreign born and trained netminder to cover for the injured Sonny Mignacca prior to the start of the Play-offs, lost all six play-off games and their future looks in doubt as the council count the cost of running a Superleague team and find it difficult to justify.

The Play-off semi finals are to be a best of three game series with each game played to a result, whilst the finals remain a one game event again held at the home of the Manchester Storm at the Nynex Arena on Saturday 28th March. In the event both semi finals only need two games to settle the finalists. The first semi-final games are played on Wednesday 18th March. Ayr beat Manchester 5-3 and Cardiff beat Sheffield 5-4. The second games of the series are played on the Saturday, Cardiff beat Sheffield 6-2 in the House of Steel whilst at the Storm Shelter the Scottish Eagles are beating the Storm 7-2. Manchester and Sheffield will play a third and fourth game before Cardiff and Ayr fight it out to be Superleague Play-off Champions. Preceding both games an England v Scotland Under19 competition is to be played.

The British National League holds its own Championship weekend at the Kingston-Upon-Hull Arena on the 21st and 22nd of March. The semi-finals are fought out on Saturday as in the days of old at Wembley. Guildford Flames put-out the Telford Tigers 5-3 and Kingston Hawks defeat the Fife Flyers 7-3. In the final on Sunday it was the Southern team again that won the final but this time the Northerns got on the score sheet as Guildford Flames beat the Kingston Hawks 5-1.

On the Manchester finals day the first goal of the Under 19 game came with 15 seconds on the clock as Colin Shields gave Scotland the first blood, and that is how the score stayed until the end of the period despite England out shooting the Scots 13-3. England's first goal was quickly followed by three more in the second period, and although Scotland scored again in the third, England were not giving up their lead and won 4-2.

During the season many commentators have noted that Ayr do not have a single British born and trained player on their bench this season. What hope have these under 19 British players of playing professional ice hockey in this country and how will the lack of British players in the Superleague affect the appeal of the game in years to come?

'Well that's tough. I wouldn't say that they need them but I think they should have them. Because I don't think the people give a monkey if we're from Canada

or not, they like the hockey. There is not a Scottish guy on this team and the fans love us, they just like to see good hockey. All the British guys in the Superleague are good players, most of them are pretty good. I don't know the whole story about Ashley Tait [cut by Nottingham and playing now for Humberside], but I don't think they should have let him go, he's not a bad player and he's British. Tait is a good player, and he could get quite a bit better, just practising with better players will help him. His speed, his passing, it all has to get better in practise. How old can he be? He could play in this league for fifteen years if he would be smart and kept practising and taking his shifts when he got them, in two or three years he could be on one of the top lines.

David Longstaff didn't get a ton of ice time in the beginning [at Sheffield], but he improved and Damps [Alex Dampier] rewarded him for it. I think some of the British guys maybe think just because they're British they deserve to play. It doesn't matter where you're from, you have just got to try to get better.

It seems like that there are no steps here [in Britain] now. It goes from kids hockey to whether you are good enough to play pro hockey with guys who are a lot better than they are. They need to be taught how to play the game when they are younger. British people know everything about soccer, like in Canada we all know about hockey, maybe the coaching is not here right now.

The British National teams can have as many imports as we do and that's all wrong. There should be three pro leagues with less and less imports on each of them so that there is a step in the quality of the league. So the British guys can step up, if they are good enough, to the better league.'

Since the Bosman ruling in the European court import rules are impossible to enforce and there would now have to be unwritten gentlemen's agreements - and a gentleman's agreement in British Ice Hockey seems a long way off.

Back to finals day at Manchester where the second game of the day, after the under19 game, was played between the two losing semi-finalists to decide third and fourth positions in the Play-Offs. The third and fourth play-off was approached with some trepidation as it could have been the most boring non-event, but as Scott said earlier in the chapter, if you are an athlete you want to win things and both teams played entertaining flowing hockey on the large ice surface. The first two periods went one apiece but in the third period Sheffield pulled away with three unanswered goals. Although it was no compensation for not being in the final, the defending Champs were the ones leaving the ice with smiles on their faces, winning the last game of the season, whatever that is, makes the summer a whole lot easier!

Most of the Manchester and Sheffield fans stayed for the final, Manchester backing Cardiff and Sheffield supporting Ayr. As with the B&H final earlier in the year, Scott felt the priority for both teams was not to make mistakes. The teams traded goals throughout the first two periods, the third failed to provide a game winning goal and the teams found themselves heading for sudden death overtime. The overtime winner was not pretty. Jamie Steer found himself behind the Cardiff goal with team mate Karry Biette in front, but the pass never made it to Biette as it was deflected into the net off the hapless Cardiff netminder's skate.

> 'It wasn't a highlight game just a solid performance. You feel a little sorry for Cardiff losing it like that. That must really spoil your summer.'

And the summer has seen some major changes to the Superleague. Although there is to be the new London Arena team called the London Knights, Basingstoke Bison have pulled out of the league. After all the fighting over the Durham Wasps with Rex Brown and then with Francis Smith for the Newcastle Arena, Sir John Hall, one of the main founding voices behind the Superleague seems to have lost interest in his Geordie Sporting Club, or at least the Ice Hockey part of it. The Superleague have stepped in to run the Newcastle Cobras team who will become the Newcastle Riverkings. Former Sheffield coach Alex Dampier will be in charge at Newcastle.

George Dodds seems to have changed his mind about spending his money on the Steelers and sweeping changes are promised in the House of Steel. The Arena has a new management company and Steelers manage to negotiate a new rental agreement. At the end of the season with the club situation in doubt the fans had got together and pledged over £100,000 and the club is looking to a possible share issue in the new season.

The ISL seems to be treading water. Leeds still do not have planning permission for their Arena and the possibility of a new team playing out of the Birmingham NEC has fallen through again.

> 'ISL needs to get stronger and better. It's not expanding - it is not getting any better. It is even getting boring for the players playing the same eight teams. The ISL should have done something to stop Basingstoke from dropping out. You've got to have stability. If the league grows and you get a major sponsor you'll attract big names from Canada, because it's English speaking. New teams, new businessmen, new sponsors are not going to be attracted with teams dropping out. No league sponsor since Heineken, that is six years in total, how hard can it be?'

Peter Woods, former Basingstoke and GB coach is to take the position of Technical Director for the Superleague as former chief referee and GB manager Nico Toeman leaves a similar role for the BIHA and returns to Holland.

But for Ayr Scottish Eagles things look rosy, the European League beckons for next season and the towns of Ayr and Prestwick have taken their heroes to heart.

> 'Our supporters are great. Our town's the smallest in the league yet 2,000 travelled for the Express Cup final on a Thursday night in Newcastle and 3,000 to the final in Manchester, that is nearly all our home support.

It seems everybody in Ayr & Prestwick knows everybody on the team but in Humberside (where Scott has also played) most people don't even know that there is an ice hockey team. Every guy on the Ayr team went in pairs and went to coach the kids right up until Christmas. All the guys went out and helped the coaches and kids. I can't walk down the street without kids saying "Hey look its Scott". Its amazing!'

Postscript

British Ice Hockey has seen so many changes in the last ten years, one of the most significant being the change in the numbers and definition of import players and the effect this has had on the British born and trained player. We have seen teams change from three professional Canadian imports playing alongside a bunch of committed amateur British players - through the rise of the professional British player, like the Coopers and Tony Hand, as the standard of play rose, but the teams still had restrictions on the number of foreigners that could play - to where we are today with teams of professional Canadians, with few opportunities available for the British player. The irony that Stevie Lyle has twice been cut from a NHL associated team due to Canadian import rules whilst more and more foreigners join our clubs at the highest level is lost on none of Britain's Ice Hockey fans. Jean-Marc Bosman might have been a footballer but his case in the European Court has affected many professional sports in the United Kingdom.

Alongside these personnel changes we have seen the sport develop off the ice as well. We have seen the demise of the small family firm, like the Durham Wasps and the local city teams like Murrayfield, changing to the big businesses like Aladdin Sports Management who have taken over Nottingham Panthers, and the Barr group who put Ayr Scottish Eagles in to the Superleague. The venues have changed alongside this. Bigger venues need more supporters to make them viable which leads to a marketing strategy where the hockey is only part of the package. With the new comfortable arenas offering a safe and comfortable environment for a family evening out the crowds have changed and grown at most venues. But big business has not guaranteed success, as the recent problems at Newcastle highlight. Likewise, despite the change to a more business orientated approach, for the first two years the Superleague failed to secure a major sponsor for the league and media coverage for any sport in the 90s is closely linked to the sponsorship it attracts.

The speed of the changes has been startling at times. The governing body and the officials have had to work hard to try to keep up. The British officials, who remain amateur, have worked hard to improve their standard but their improvements have, at times, not kept pace with the huge leaps in the game. The BIHA found the changes meant that too much of their time was being taken up by the new professional teams, (lawsuits becoming the normal response to player suspensions and fines), drawing resources away from the smaller teams and the development of the national teams. Their response was to facilitate the arrival of the Superleague, allowing the big businesses to manage themselves whilst the BIHA focused on the rest of the sport. Superleague has had to learn and adapt quickly as the big business of sport is still considered important enough for the teams that run the league to resort to the law when decisions do not go favourably for them.

We have seen the Great Britain team change and develop as well. Through the ten years they have risen from Pool D to the dizzy heights of Pool A for one season before finding their level at Pool B. Whether the national team can maintain this high standard whilst the British born and trained players fail to make it on to the teams at the highest level domestically, only time will tell us.

There is plenty in British Ice Hockey for the pessimists to worry about and plenty for the optimists to build on. If the last ten years is an indicator of anything it just goes to show that there is a constant ebb and flow which makes the current direction of the tide hard to follow. As one team in the league takes a giant leap forward another can be found dropping back.

Whatever else happens in the future of British Ice Hockey, the sport will continue to rely on the quality and professionalism of the players employed. The leagues must ensure that the high standard of skill, commitment and character demonstrated by those interviewed for this book is maintained and developed for the good of the game. So book your seat and climb on board for the next ten years of British Ice Hockey.